# EMPOWERED TEAMS

# *Empowered* TEAMS

CREATING
SELF-DIRECTED
WORK GROUPS
THAT IMPROVE
QUALITY,
PRODUCTIVITY,
AND PARTICIPATION

RICHARD S. WELLINS
WILLIAM C. BYHAM
JEANNE M. WILSON

Jossey-Bass Publishers · San Francisco

**EMPOWERED TEAMS**
*Creating Self-Directed Work Groups That Improve Quality,*
*Productivity, and Participation*

by Richard S. Wellins, William C. Byham, and Jeanne M. Wilson

Copyright © 1991 by: Jossey-Bass Inc., Publishers
350 Sansome Street
San Francisco, California 94104

&

Jossey-Bass Limited
Headington Hill Hall
Oxford OX3 0BW

**Library of Congress Cataloging-in-Publication Data**
Wellins, Richard S.
    Empowered teams : creating self-directed work groups that improve quality, productivity, and participation / Richard S. Wellins, William C. Byham, Jeanne M. Wilson.
        p.  cm. — (The Jossey-Bass management series)
    Includes bibliographical references and index.
    ISBN 1-55542-353-1
    1. Work groups.  I. Byham, William C.  II. Wilson, Jeanne M.,
1957–    .  III. Title.  IV. Series.
HD66.W45  1991
658.4′02—dc20                                                           91-9880
                                                                              CIP

Manufactured in the United States of America

The paper used in this book is acid-free and meets the State of California requirements for recycled paper (50 percent recycled waste, including 10 percent post-consumer waste), which are the strictest guidelines for recycled paper currently in use in the United States.

A BARD PRODUCTIONS BOOK

Copy Editing/Proofreading: Helen Hyams
Text Design: Suzanne Pustejovsky
Jacket Design: Suzanne Pustejovsky
Composition/Production: Round Rock Graphics
Indexing: Linda Webster

FIRST EDITION

*HB Printing*        10 9 8 7 6 5 4 3

*Code 9157*

*The Jossey-Bass*
*Management Series*

———

# CONTENTS

# TABLES

# FIGURES

# PREFACE

W e wrote this book to quench the thirst for knowledge that may have drawn you to the title *Empowered Teams: Creating Self-Directed Work Groups That Improve Quality, Productivity, and Participation.* You may have heard about the success of self-directed teams. Many of you have visited organizations where you have seen teams in action and wondered if they would work in your organization. Or you may have piloted teams elsewhere in your organization and are now ready to try them out in your division or plant. Wherever your interests lie, this book can help you learn more about the role self-directed work teams will play in keeping your organization competitive.

Self-directed work teams are small groups of people empowered to manage themselves and the work they do on a day-to-day basis. They are different from other types of teams or "teamwork" you may be using currently in your organization in that self-directed teams are formal, permanent organizational structures or units that perform and manage work. Typically, members of self-directed work teams not only handle their job responsibilities but also plan and schedule their work, make production-related decisions, take action to solve problems, and share leadership responsibilities.

Self-directed teams are not a panacea. Their implementation should be tied to clear business needs, and they may not fit with your organizational culture. Yet we *do* believe empowered teams can be a strong part of your overall competitive strategy. Our confidence is based on three assumptions:

1. Those closest to the work know best how to perform and improve their jobs.

2. Most employees want to feel that they "own" their jobs and are making meaningful contributions to the effectiveness of their organizations.

3. Teams provide possibilities for empowerment that are not available to individual employees.

Over the past thirty years, hundreds of books and articles have been written about team dynamics, group cohesiveness, and high-performance teams. Recently, several excellent books have appeared that contain chapters or sections on self-directed teams (Lawler, 1986; Hackman, 1989). The popular press has picked up on the excitement as well (Dumaine, 1990; Hoerr, 1989a; Lee, 1990).

To date, however, no single source has attempted to address some of the key questions and issues we hear from organizations that are considering the implementation of teams:

- What are self-directed work teams, and how are they different from traditional teams?

- How can we tell if self-directed work teams will work in our organization?

- How do we go about starting self-directed work teams?

- How can we keep our existing self-directed work teams going?

We wrote this book to answer these questions (and many more), with the goal of helping those organizations that are exploring the feasibility of self-directed work teams and those that are facing the many challenges of a work team implementation. In short, *Empowered Teams* is meant to serve as a blueprint for successful team implementation within your workplace.


## Sources of Information

Hundreds of organizations have successfully implemented self-directed teams (and a few have been unsuccessful as well). In writing this book, we wanted to rely heavily on what these organizations had to offer. Toward this end, our book is based on four general sources of information:

1. *A national survey.* As a separate but related effort to writing this book, we conducted and published the results of a survey of more than 500 organizations that are now using self-directed teams. We conducted this survey in conjunction with *Industry Week* and the Association for Quality and Participation. Throughout the book we share these data and reference the source as the "Survey" (Wellins and others, 1990). The appendix describes the research methodology for this study in greater depth.

2. *Research.* As part of the research base for this book, we conducted interviews with twenty-eight organizations that used self-directed work teams. We chose a comprehensive representation of companies based on size, location, and industry type, both white and blue collar. Our research included dozens of site visits

and a number of "focus groups," involving the people responsible for implementing work teams in their organizations.

3. *Review of the literature.* We conducted an extensive literature search, reviewing more than 100 separate articles and books. We have included an extensive reference section and a separate annotated bibliography for those who want to learn more about teams.

4. *Experience.* We have assisted numerous companies in making the work team transition. Our areas of expertise include culture change, organizational design, selection, and training. We have also implemented work teams within our own organization at our printing facility and distribution center.

## A Map of This Book

*Empowered Teams* is designed for a varied audience. The book contains useful information for those who are eager to examine the potential of teams or who are concerned with nurturing and developing their current implementations. The book is targeted at executives, line managers, and human resource executives who are responsible for bringing the team vision to their organizations. However, facilitators, first-line leaders, and team members—those who are involved with teams on a day-to-day basis—will also benefit from reading the book. *Empowered Teams* can serve as a guide for steering committee and design team members as they make important decisions that will shape how teams look in their organizations. Finally, we've included examples from manufacturing and service organizations, companies with and without union affiliations, and both "start-ups" and existing organizations so that readers can see how self-directed work teams operate in situations similar to theirs.

The book starts with a prologue: "A Workplace Revolution: The Coming of Empowered Teams." In the prologue, we define teams, show how they are developed, and review why they are so important today—to both individuals and organizations.

The thirteen chapters following the prologue are divided into three parts. The first part, Chapters One through Four, serves readers who do not yet have much experience with teams and offers fresh insights to those who do. It describes what teams are and how they work.

Chapter One focuses on "Empowering Teams." Here we introduce the *team empowerment continuum*, which suggests the direction of team growth and tracks the acquisition of responsibility in a team. Chapter Two, "Moving Toward Empowered Teams," shows how a reshuffling of leadership roles takes place as companies move from traditional, supervisor-centered organizations to self-directed teams. In Chapter Three, "Confronting New Organizational Questions," some of the characteristics and practices of work teams are explored. Using the Survey findings, we see how similar—and how different—existing teams are. Chapter Four, "A Day in the Life of a Self-Directed Team," takes a closeup look at one team and observes how it operates.

The second part, Chapters Five through Nine, deals with the actual mechanics of starting and maintaining teams. These chapters are more appropriate for those who are seeking guidance through the early stages of a work team implementation or who are faced with the challenge of keeping their teams going. With this in mind, we have included "Team Tips" sections at the conclusion of each of these chapters, which offer practical advice on team installation and maintenance.

In Chapter Five, "Implementing a New Vision," we look at ways to create a vision and culture that are conducive to developing teams. We explain how teams fit in with overall business strategy. This chapter includes a self-analysis instrument to help you determine your organization's readiness for teams. Chapter Six, "Planning the Successful Launch of Self-Directed Teams," describes the process for designing and implementing teams, both in start-ups and in established organizations. Chapter Seven, "The New Look of Leadership," adds more clarity to the role of leaders in the team setting.

Because some employees are better suited than others to the self-directed work team environment, Chapter Eight, "Selecting Team Players," addresses the issue of what to look for when choosing team members, team leaders, and group leaders. Chapter Nine covers another essential element of success, "Training the New Team." Our own research, coupled with data from the Survey, indicates that insufficient training is the leading cause of team failure. In this chapter, we present a typical training plan for team members and leaders and show you how to develop your own.

The third part, which consists of Chapters Ten through Thirteen, talks about the four developmental stages of teams: Getting Started, Going in Circles, Getting on Course, and Full Speed Ahead. In these chapters we present the "feel" of a team at each particular stage and offer tips for advancing from one stage to the next.

We close with an epilogue, "What's Next for Self-Directed Teams?" in which we provide data relating to the expected emergence of work teams and consider broader issues that are facing the growth of teams worldwide.

## Writing as a Team Effort

This book represents a team effort. We decided that since *Empowered Teams* is *about* teams, it should be written *by* a team. Here are some of the obstacles we faced:

- Writing a book is a major effort, especially when all the authors are busy maintaining regular work schedules.

- We all have different bases of knowledge and different feelings about work teams.

- Each of us has our own style. Yet our mission required us to write *one* book, not a collection of individual chapters.

- Authoring is a creative effort, which further tests a team concept.

And here are the outcomes:

- We all learned more about self-directed teams and how to work effectively as a team.

- The team process allowed us to build upon each other's ideas and experiences. The whole became more than the sum of its parts.

- The organizations that are implementing teams represent a group of pioneers who truly believe in a new way of looking at work. We developed a great deal of respect for these pioneers.

We believe that self-directed teams will become the standard—not the exception—within the next decade. We hope that you will benefit from *Empowered Teams* as you successfully implement self-directed teams in your organizations. The journey is a long one with few shortcuts. But getting there can be fun. And once you've arrived, the payoffs can be tremendous.

*Pittsburgh, Pennsylvania*      Richard S. Wellins
*April 1991*      William C. Byham
      Jeanne M. Wilson

# ACKNOWLEDGMENTS

The team that turned this book into a reality extended far beyond the three of us. We wish to thank those individuals who provided us with both inspirational and professional support throughout the year and a half we worked on *Empowered Teams*.

First, for taking a document written by three authors with very different writing styles and turning it into a book, we thank Robert Matzen, Kathy Shomo, and Dan Siemasko. Their patience endured—even after the eleventh draft—and we appreciate their objectivity and valuable input.

Bill Hicks, our Jossey-Bass editor, and Ray Bard, Helen Hyams, and Suzanne Pustejovsky of Bard Productions made numerous suggestions to improve the quality of the manuscript and were always there with a word of encouragement. Chuck Day, editor of *Indus-*

*try Week,* and Amy Katz and Patricia Laughlin of the Association for Quality and Participation were our partners in the survey research referenced throughout this book. Without their help and support, there would have been no data to share.

Several colleagues reviewed our manuscript and offered insightful comments. We thank Alan Cheney, a member of the Corporate Leadership Development Center at Texas Instruments; Susan Conway, plant manager at Sara Lee Knit Products; Nick Grabar, consultant, organization development, at Eastman Chemical Company; Ron Mitchell, a work teams consultant and colleague; and Judy Robinson, personnel manager at Schreiber Foods.

We also wish to express our gratitude to our DDI support team. Background research, project coordination, editing, graphics, word processing, and dozens of other tasks were performed with the usual diligence and high work standards we've come to expect—and appreciate! Our thanks to Tammy Bercosky, Nancy Boyle, Sharon Cambest, Darla Cronin, Jeanette Fagnelli, Mary Holden, Helene Lautman, Marcia Medvid, Doreen Price, and Lynne Weber. Jill George and Larry Holpp, also from DDI, contributed to many of the models presented in the book and provided thoughtful review—more than once.

Finally, dozens of organizations and their team associates openly shared with us their trials and joys as they moved toward teams. They serve as models for the rest of us, and we wish them the best.

R.S.W.
W.C.B.
J.M.W.

# THE AUTHORS

**Richard S. Wellins** is senior vice-president of programs and marketing for Development Dimensions International (DDI), a human resource consulting firm headquartered in Pittsburgh, Pennsylvania, with offices around the world. He received his B.A. degree (1973) in psychology, his M.A. degree (1975) in experimental and social psychology, and his Ph.D. degree (1977) in applied social psychology, all from American University.

Since joining DDI more than a decade ago, Rich has focused much of his time in the areas of new program development, research, and consulting. Recently, Rich formed DDI's Start-Up Group, a team of professionals dedicated to creating high-involvement work cultures. The group specializes in organizational design, selection, and training. Start-Up clients include Colgate-Palmolive Company, Hershey Foods Corporation, Toyota Motor Corporation, and NCR Corporation.

Rich has published and presented more than thirty papers and articles concerning selection, work teams, and customer service. Recently he led a research team that published *Self-Directed Teams: A Study of Current Practice* (Wellins, Wilson, Katz, Laughlin, and Day, 1990), a major study involving more than 500 organizations.

**William C. Byham** is cofounder and president of DDI. An internationally known educator, consultant, and speaker, he is the author of more than 100 articles, papers, and books. He received his B.S. degree (1958) and M.S. degree (1959) from Ohio University in science and his Ph.D. degree (1962) from Purdue University in industrial/organizational psychology.

Bill has received numerous awards for his innovative training technologies and for his commitment to research on the effectiveness of DDI programs. In 1989 he received the Professional Practice Award from the Society of Industrial and Organizational Psychology of the American Psychological Association, and in 1988 he was awarded the Distinguished Contribution to Human Resource Development Award from the American Society for Training and Development. He is past president of the Instructional Systems Association.

Bill is the author of *Zapp! The Lightning of Empowerment* (1990) and coauthor of *Assessment Centers and Managerial Performance* (1982, with G. Thornton) and *Applying the Assessment Center Method* (1977, with J. Moses).

**Jeanne M. Wilson** is project manager for high-involvement clients at DDI. She received her B.S. degree (1979) from St. Joseph's College, Indiana, in psychology and her M.S. degree (1982) from Purdue University in industrial/organizational psychology.

In her seven years with DDI, Jeanne has concentrated on consulting projects in team development, quality improvement, culture change, and empowerment. She helps numerous clients implement team design and selection systems. Some of these clients include Colgate-Palmolive Company, Subaru-Isuzu Automotive, Valeo Engine Cooling, I/N Tek (an Inland Steel Industries and Nippon Steel joint venture), and Becton, Dickinson and Company. She also plans and designs team training systems for organizations such as Airwick and Amoco Corporation.

Jeanne recently completed a nationwide survey of self-directed team practices and coauthored articles based on the results.

# A Workplace Revolution:
## The Coming of
## Empowered Teams

**D**riving into the plant parking lot this morning, Tom Marshall is bothered with thoughts of a supplier who isn't meeting standards.

Tom considers the situation as he walks to the door; in the future they are going to have to be a lot more careful with the products they buy. Going to total quality means a big change, and the company almost lost an important customer last week as a result of this supplier's practices. Tom knows how sensitive his customers have been recently to the slightest variations in product, so today he must confront the supplier about the problem.

As he goes through the door, he remembers everything that has to be done on his shift. This morning's schedule says that his unit will run at least ten different configurations. There might be more, depending on business. The implementation of his company's Flexible Manufacturing Program has made it difficult to set schedules. He can think back to two or three years ago when a special configuration could require a customer to wait more than a month.

Tom is pleased as he walks down the line because work is already moving ahead; Linda, a new associate, has started early. As he checks the front end, he sees a slight problem, but no reason for undue alarm. It could be a slight temperature or timing problem, or it could be the supplier's materials acting up again. He makes a mental note of possible causes and then starts to work on his morning reports.

About an hour later, Linda approaches Tom for help. Tom devotes about twenty minutes to Linda and coaches her on the finer points of temperature control. Tom knows how tricky all these adjustments are to a new person because he was in the same spot a few years ago when the line was installed.

At midday Tom glances at the unit's production figures and is pleased to note that things are going well. All five variables are within tolerance. No more operating problems. He glances at his watch; it's time for the morning production meeting.

First up at the meeting is a discussion about hiring a new person. A consensus is reached on the best applicant. Next on the agenda is the supplier with the quality problem. Tom pushes for a meeting with the supplier and suggests offering the supplier training in statistical process control.

If you were to follow Tom around, you would think he was a production supervisor or a plant manager—until you saw him putting in time on the line, operating the controls, and changing setups. Tom Marshall is a member of one of twenty work teams at this plant. Although individual participation varies, most team members are like Tom, more engaged in their work than they or their organizations ever could have imagined.

Ask Tom about the difference work teams have made in his life and he'll tell you how rewarding work teams are—for him, his co-workers, and the company. He'll also tell you how much better he feels using his head now, instead of just his hands. "It used to be," he says, "that nothing we said or did would change anything around here. I'd be working and thinking about all the things I could be doing at home, or about how bored I was. Now my mind is with me, my co-workers are with me, and we're actually having a good time. And the numbers prove our company's healthier for it, too."

## WHAT IS A SELF-DIRECTED WORK TEAM?

A *self-directed work team* is an intact group of employees who are responsible for a "whole" work process or segment that delivers a product or service to an internal or external customer. To varying degrees, team members work together to improve their operations, handle day-to-day problems, and plan and control their work. In other words, they are responsible not only for getting work done but also for managing themselves.

Several characteristics typically distinguish self-directed teams from other types of teams. First, as our definition states, a self-directed work team is an intact group of people who normally work together on an ongoing, day-to-day basis. It is not a group brought together for a special purpose, such as a product-launch team, a quality-action team, or a quality circle.

Second, work is usually designed to give the team "owner-ship" of a product or service. In manufacturing environments, a team might be responsible for a whole product or a clearly defined segment of the production process. At Tennessee Eastman, a division of Eastman Kodak Company, teams are responsible for manufacturing entire "product lines," including processing, lab work, and packaging. Similarly, in a service environment, the team usually has responsibility for entire groupings of products and ser-vices, often serving clients in a designated geographic area. For example, Aid Association for Lutherans (AAL), a fraternal benefits society in the top 2 percent of all life insurers, has combined separate life insurance, health insurance, and support service func-tions into teams that handle all these tasks for clients in specific regional areas. Providing this type of ownership usually requires broader job categories and the sharing of work assignments. Rather than mastering one narrow job or task, team members may be expected, at various times, to perform all the jobs of the team.

Among the distinguishing characteristics of self-directed teams are the following:

- They are empowered to share various management and leadership functions.

- They plan, control, and improve their own work processes.

- They set their own goals and inspect their own work.

- They often create their own schedules and review their per-formance as a group.

- They may prepare their own budgets and coordinate their work with other departments.

- They usually order materials, keep inventories, and deal with suppliers.

- They frequently are responsible for acquiring any new train-ing they might need.

- They may hire their own replacements or assume responsibility for disciplining their own members.

- They—not others outside the team—take responsibility for the quality of their products or services.

Table P.1 summarizes some of the key differences between a traditional organization and an organization that uses self-directed work teams. While there are several alternatives that will take organizations beyond traditional top-to-bottom structures, work teams go well beyond past attempts at employee involvement. Typically, team members move from more passive and reactive roles to more proactive ones. By assuming authority over their work, self-directed work team members become actively involved in the process of continuous improvement. Teams engage members in a spirit of cooperation, information sharing, flexibility, and fulfillment different from that of most other organizations.

## WHERE DID WORK TEAMS COME FROM?

Teamwork is not a new concept. Americans have cheered on their teams practically since the first boatload of Pilgrims arrived. Yet as dearly as we hold on to our romantic notions of teams, the team concept has tended to stay "in its place"—on playing fields, in films, and through the use of stale clichés.

We may talk about the value of teamwork with our children, but much of the real world they see is oriented toward the individual. We are proud of our children when they hit home runs; we urge students to compete for individual recognition through high grades. And when work begins, performance systems continue to reward individual accomplishments. All through life we celebrate the individual. Unfortunately, Tom Marshall's experience with teamwork is foreign to most organizations.

**TABLE P.1**
**Key Differences Between Traditional Organizations**
**and Empowered Team Organizations**

| Element | Traditional Organizations | Self-Directed Teams |
|---|---|---|
| Organizational structure | Layered/individual | Flat/team |
| Job design | Narrow single-task | Whole process/ multiple-task |
| Management role | Direct/control | Coach/facilitate |
| Leadership | Top-down | Shared with team |
| Information flow | Controlled/limited | Open/shared |
| Rewards | Individual/seniority | Team-based/skills-based |
| Job process | Managers plan, control, improve | Teams plan, control, improve |

With teamwork so ambiguous a value in the American culture, it's no wonder we're having trouble implementing the concept in industry today. We're trying to build on a foundation that is anything but firm.

Why haven't Americans organized their work more around the team concept? When you ask this question, many experts point to Frederick Taylor, the father of modern industrial engineering. It was Taylor who, at the turn of the century, recommended that the best way to manage manufacturing organizations was to standardize the activity of general workers into simple, repetitive tasks and then closely supervise them (Taylor, 1947).

At the time, it seemed to make sense to mechanize the activity of the general work force and to leave the decision making, coordinating, and controlling to the authorities at the top of the pyramid. In effect, management did all the thinking and employees did all the doing. In his book *High-Involvement Management* (1986), University of Southern California business professor Dr. Edward E. Lawler III notes that the assembly line idea was ready-made for an American work force composed of poorly educated immigrants who, in many cases, did not speak English.

As manufacturing systems picked up speed, organizations divided by functions and job specialties, managers made all the decisions, and supervisors—the watchers—became better at calling out orders and controlling work. The workers focused on doing what they were told. Input from employees was thought to slow things down. Besides, managers had no time to listen to or consider workers' ideas; there were system-wide efficiencies to maintain. Factories were large machines, and people were no more than small cogs in those machines.

In a culture based on independence, an ironic thing happened. Many workers were forced to surrender their independence and the freedom they had enjoyed as members of small, craft-based teams. The captains of industry operated on a model that was large scale, high volume, and machine paced. Central control became more important than individual autonomy. Power reverted back into the hands of a few leaders, and workers gave up control and ownership of their work in the move toward a new way of getting things done.

Although centralizing power may have made sense at the time, the regrettable result was a loss of worker empowerment. For nearly a century, millions of American workers performed with little sense of ownership, participation, or control.

While American organizations busily exercised high-control management and slowly lost their competitive positions, some early experiments in self-direction proceeded abroad. For example, in the early 1950s, Eric Trist (1981), now professor emeritus at the Wharton School, was conducting research on British coal miners. Some miners were formed into teams based on an analysis of the technical and social requirements of their jobs (a process that later became known as *sociotechnical design*). In the mines, employees worked together, helping each other and often trading jobs. Trist discovered clear indications of higher productivity and job satisfaction among those workers who were given more control of their jobs. Trist's studies also indicated that organizations with workers who were more involved in the operation were better equipped to respond to changing market and political conditions—something that large and rigid organizations found difficult.

Sweden also experimented with fresh approaches to work design, the most notable at the Volvo Corporation plant in Kalmar (Katz and Kahn, 1978). Instead of building a factory that would support traditional assembly line manufacturing, Volvo built a new plant that ferried cars around on mechanical carriers to different teams of workers, who were responsible for putting together entire units such as electrical or transmission systems. Volvo's team approach became an intrinsic part of the workplace, resulting in both greater morale *and* a 25 percent reduction in production costs compared with Volvo's conventional plants. Volvo's newest plant in Uddevalla eliminated the assembly line altogether, creating instead a facility consisting of six "workshops" organized around a central parts warehouse. Teams in the workshops build entire cars (Johnson, 1989).

In the meantime, American management began a long—and still ongoing—journey toward greater employee involvement. It started in the early 1960s with the Quality of Worklife movement, where managers and supervisors first asked employees for ideas that would make their jobs easier and more pleasant. Although this resulted in temporary improvements in morale and worker attitudes, many skeptics complained that the only long-term impact was a fresh coat of paint on the factory's walls.

In the late 1970s, employee involvement groups called *quality circles* began to take hold. They originated in Japan, and their aim was to suggest ways of improving quality and cutting costs. Quality circles are groups of employees who work together on specific quality, productivity, and service problems. These groups usually consist of members from different parts of the organization; during the height of their popularity, some companies operated hundreds of circles simultaneously. Although quality circles are considered by some to have fallen by the wayside, they served an important purpose: Value was placed on workers' opinions, and recognition was given for work-related input and decisions— with some impressive results. Perhaps more important, the value of teamwork became far more prominent. However, quality circles often experienced the problem of being only temporary in nature; in addition, although circle members were asked to come up with solutions, they rarely had the power and authority to transform their ideas into action (Sundstrom, Demeuse, and Futrell, 1990).

The application of self-direction didn't really begin in the United States until the mid 1960s to early 1970s, with a handful of pioneers like the Procter & Gamble Company and the famous Gaines dog food plant in Topeka, Kansas (Ketchum, 1984). The concept began to spread during the 1970s, but at a snail's pace. It wasn't until the mid 1980s that self-directed teams caught on— like wildfire.

Data from the national Survey we conducted with *Industry Week* and the Association for Quality and Participation indicate that today, one-fourth of the organizations in North America are at least experimenting with self-directed work teams, and those organizations are expected to expand their use of teams rapidly. (Throughout the book this source is referred to as the "Survey." See the appendix for a detailed description of the Survey methodology.) Large manufacturing companies like Xerox Corporation, Milliken & Co., Best Foods, General Electric Company, IBM Corporation, Corning, Digital Equipment Corporation, Colgate-Palmolive Company, and TRW are implementing teams. Smaller companies like Johnsonville Foods and Lake Superior Paper Industries have embraced the team concept so powerfully that they too serve as models for other companies. Meanwhile, white-collar and service organizations like AT&T and AAL are making progress in their journey toward self-direction.

Is self-direction an idea whose time has come? In the fall of 1990, Texas Instruments and the University of North Texas sponsored the first International Conference on Self-Managed Work Teams. They expected only 90 attendees; when registrations reached 350, they had to turn people away.

## TODAY'S MOVE TOWARD TEAMS

Why are so many of today's organizations looking to work teams? This change is taking place because more people are realizing that empowered teams provide a way to accomplish organizational goals and meet the needs of our changing work force.

As plants, hospitals, service organizations, and American businesses as a whole seek to become more efficient, they cannot overlook the advantages offered by flexible, self-disciplined, multiskilled work teams. Meanwhile, workers recognize the benefits inherent in the self-directed work environment: an opportunity to participate, to learn different job skills, and to feel like a valuable part of their organizations.

Table P.2, based on data from the Survey, shows the top reasons senior line managers give for their organizations' movement toward self-directed teams. Some of these and other reasons for establishing teams are elaborated on next.

*Improved quality, productivity, and service.* To stay competitive, today's organizations must bundle service, quality, speed, and cost containment into one package. Success in these areas seldom comes from giant leaps; rather, it comes from thousands of small steps taken by individuals at all levels in the organization. Technical breakthroughs are one thing, but day-to-day work enhancements to both product and process have proven an even greater catalyst. The Japanese call it *kaizen:* continuous improvement. The sense

**TABLE P.2**
**Primary Reasons Cited for Moving Toward Self-Directed Teams**

| Cited as Primary Reason | Respondents (%) |
| --- | --- |
| Quality | 38 |
| Productivity | 22 |
| Reduced operating costs | 17 |
| Job satisfaction | 12 |
| Restructuring | 5 |
| Other | 6 |

*Source:* Wellins, Wilson, Katz, Laughlin, and Day, 1990.

of job ownership resulting from the team concept has led to an emphasis on continuous improvement, which in turn has led to amazing leaps in quality, productivity, and service.

*Greater flexibility.*   Advances in service quality today rely heavily on an organization's ability to discover ways of increasing its responsiveness to customers and the marketplace—the days of the "standard model" are long over. In searching for ways to adapt more quickly, many companies are realizing the inherent advantages of work teams. Teams can communicate better, tackle more opportunities, find better solutions, and implement actions more quickly. Many teams in manufacturing environments are organized into work "cells," which reorganize in a fluid way to accommodate shifting demands in production. Because of the nature of teams, their members are often more engaged, alert, proactive, knowledgeable, and generally better able to respond to varying conditions than traditionally organized work forces.

*Reduced operating costs.*   To remain competitive, many companies have been forced to eliminate layers of middle-level management and supervision. For example, North American automotive plants used to have ten or more layers of management. In order to compete with other countries today, however, they are learning to run their plants with four or five layers. With fewer managers, many decisions must be made at lower levels. Empowered teams provide a vehicle for employees to take on the responsibilities typically reserved for managers or supervisors.

*Faster response to technological change.*   Today's advanced manufacturing technologies call for different and usually higher worker skills. These technologies also create closer interdependence among activities that were once separate; thus, workers who previously worked alone now must learn to work together. Also, as production processes become more closely linked, they become more sensitive to variations. At the same time, the consequences of a malfunction are more costly. Teams provide the communication links and responsiveness necessary to make advanced technology work (Walton, 1985).

*Fewer, simpler job classifications.*   As technology becomes more complex and the need for flexibility grows, many organizations see a corresponding need for multiskilled individuals who can perform many different job functions. There was a time when twenty-five distinct job classifications may have been appropriate for a given production process, each filled with one or two employees. Today, employees are asked to perform several functions, often rotating and filling in for one another. Teams are designed to facilitate job sharing and cross-training.

*Better response to new worker values.*   Employees today welcome the autonomy, responsibility, and empowerment that self-directed teams provide. The results of a recent Louis Harris poll, as reported in the *Behavioral Sciences Newsletter,* show that of all employees who were asked, "Do you want the freedom to decide how to do your work?" 77 percent answered "yes." Employees reported that factors such as the challenge of the task, participation in decision making, and work that gives a feeling of accomplishment are more important than high levels of pay ("What Workers Want," 1988). Those values and "wants" are wholly consistent with the empowered team concept.

*Ability to attract and retain the best people.* Labor statisticians predict that in the coming decade, there will be sixteen million new jobs in America, with only fourteen million people available to fill them. *Workplace Basics* (Carnevale, Gainer, and Meltzer, 1988), an excellent report on the changing work force, points out that "American employers will no longer be able to select from a field of workers with strong basic skills" (p. 1). The job crunch is on the way!

Organizations that acquire (and retain) capable work forces will offer a culture that matches the values of the new work forces previously discussed. Teams offer greater participation, challenge, and feelings of accomplishment. Organizations with teams will attract and retain the best people. The others will have to do without.

## EXAMPLES OF WORK TEAMS' SUCCESS

Perhaps the biggest reason for the movement toward empowered work teams is the fact that *teams work*. The results of self-directed work teams are inspiring many organizations to experiment and become involved. More and more organizations are demonstrating that work teams *do* improve quality, customer service, and productivity. They reduce costs and boost morale. *Business Week* reports that plants designed with sociotechnical methods and using self-directed work teams are, on average, 30 to 50 percent more productive than their conventional counterparts (Hoerr and Pollock, 1986).

Here are some other results attributed to teams, as reported in recent literature:

- Shenandoah Life Insurance Company in Roanoke, Virginia, reduced staffing needs, yielding a savings of $200,000 per year. During this same period, the volume of work handled increased by 33 percent (O'Dell, 1989).

- Westinghouse Furniture Systems increased productivity by 74 percent in three years (Hoerr, 1987).

- AAL increased productivity by 20 percent. As part of this productivity gain, the company cut personnel by 10 percent, while handling 10 percent more transactions (Hoerr, 1988).

- Federal Express Corporation cut service errors (such as lost packages) by 13 percent (Dumaine, 1990).

- Carrier, a division of United Technologies Corporation, reduced unit turnaround time in its new Georgia facility from two weeks to two days (Wysocki, 1990).

- Volvo Corporation's Kalmar facility reduced defects by 90 percent (Patinkin, 1987).

- General Electric Company's Salisbury, North Carolina, plant increased productivity by 250 percent compared with other GE plants producing the same products (Hoerr, 1989b).

- Corning's new specialty cellular ceramics plant decreased defect rates from 1,800 parts per million to 9 parts per million (Sheridan, 1990).

- General Mills' plants that use teams are as much as 40 percent more productive than their plants operating without teams (Dumaine, 1990).

- AT&T's Richmond, Virginia, operator service increased service quality by 12 percent (Wesner and Egan, 1990).

- Dana Corporation's Minneapolis, Minnesota, valve plant trimmed customer lead time from six months to six weeks (Sheridan, 1990).

In addition to these impressive results, self-directed teams have begun to spark serious academic investigation. For example, Near and Weckler of San Jose State University (1990) compared self-directed teams with traditional structures on a number of organizational and job characteristics. Not surprisingly, self-directed team members scored significantly higher than their traditional counterparts on the following factors: innovation, information sharing, employee involvement, and task/job significance. Similarly, Macy, Norton, Bliese, and Izumi (1990) completed an analysis of work design efforts across seventy organizations. The researchers found that self-directed teams correlated very highly with financial and behavioral outcomes such as increased organizational effectiveness, heightened productivity, and reduced defects.

While work team results are largely positive, we offer one word of caution: Most of the results we reported were provided by organizations that not only have made the move toward self-direction but also have reorganized work flow, significantly increased training, brought in new technologies, or implemented new production and quality processes. For this reason, it is difficult to separate the impact of self-directed teams from other changes.

Nevertheless, the volume of success stories makes it difficult to ignore the potential power of self-directed teams. Self-directed teams change the way people look at their work. The majority of team members we interviewed enjoy the ownership and empowerment that accompanies the team concept. It is a feeling many have never experienced before in the workplace!

# PART

# I

# How Teams Work

A s explained in the prologue, self-directed teams are truly different from work forces in traditional organizations, and from other forms of employee involvement and teamwork.

The next four chapters cover the "inner workings" of teams. We start in Chapter One by positioning teams within the broader context of organizational empowerment. Teams provide organizations with a viable way of increasing empowerment and job ownership that is unavailable in individual jobs. Next, in Chapter Two, we discuss the shift of leadership responsibility from formal leaders, supervisors, and managers to the team itself. It is this shift that really sets empowered teams apart. A team becomes a mini-enterprise responsible for getting the job done, managing itself, and working directly with internal (and perhaps external) customers and suppliers.

In Chapter Three, we try to answer questions often posed by those who are considering teams. We cover the nature of team compensation, multiskilling, ideal team size, the role of the union, how support functions are handled, and a number of other key issues. The answers to these questions are based on a combination of the Survey and our own research and interviews with dozens of team-based organizations.

In Chapter Four, we close this part by describing in detail a "day in the life" of a real team in a food-processing facility, providing a better feel for what it's like to work as a team member in an empowered organization.

# EMPOWERING TEAMS:

## Reaping the Benefits of Greater Employee Participation

Two "Help Wanted" ads showed up in the same newspaper on the same Sunday, on the same page, side by side. Both came from automotive companies seeking maintenance personnel, but no one planned their side-by-side placement—it was pure coincidence. Figure 1.1 shows how they appeared.

It is difficult to believe that these ads represent the same type of position in the same industry. Although the facilities

## Our Team Needs One Good
## Multiskilled Maintenance Associate

Our team is down one good player. Join our group of multiskilled Maintenance Associates who work together to support our assembly teams at American Automotive Manufacturing.

We are looking for a versatile person with skills in one or more of the following: ability to set up and operate various welding machinery, knowledge in electric arc and M.I.G. welding, willingness to work on detailed projects for extended time periods, and general overall knowledge of the automobile manufacturing process. Willingness to learn all maintenance skills a must. You must be a real team player, have excellent interpersonal skills, and be motivated to work in a highly participative environment.

Send qualifications to:

AAM

American Automotive Manufacturing
P.O. Box 616
Ft. Wayne, Indiana 48606

Include phone number. We respond to all applicants.

## Maintenance Technician/Welder

Leading automotive manufacturer looking for Maintenance Technician/Welder. Position requires the ability to set up and operate various welding machinery and a general knowledge of the automobile production process. Vocational school graduates or 3-5 years of on-the-job experience required. Competitive salary, full benefits, and tuition reimbursement offered.

Interviews Monday, May 6, at the Holiday Inn South, 3000 Semple Road, 9:00 a.m. to 7:00 p.m. Please bring pay stub as proof of last employment.

NMC

National Motors Corporation
5169 Blane Hill Center
Springfield, Illinois 62707

**Figure 1.1.** Team employment advertisement and traditional employment advertisement.

sit just 300 miles apart, in some ways they look as if they exist in different worlds. One still operates as a traditional organization; the other uses self-directed work teams.

The employees in the work team facility helped to design their own jobs. They determined their own mission statement and values, which are proudly posted in the facility's work area. There is a spirit of ownership and responsibility in their ad, which they wrote themselves. Clearly they are interested in filling the position with the right person; they know exactly what the position requires, and they will, in fact, have the final say in whom they hire.

The other, more formal ad comes from a company where most day-to-day decision making and control still reside at the top. The supervisor with the vacancies wrote this job description more than eight years ago, following the directions in a manual provided by Personnel. All he had to do when he wanted new workers was to pull the job file, make a copy of the job description, and pass the paperwork up the line—to the floor supervisor, department head, section manager, and plant manager. Someone in Personnel plugged the job description into the company's standard "Help Wanted" format and sent it to the *Post*.

Which type of "Help Wanted" ad does your company run?

## EMPOWERING INDIVIDUALS

The difference in the want ads in Figure 1.1 is telling. It speaks of movement, direction, and an evolution toward empowerment.

Most organizations believe that a commitment to continuous improvement by all members is a must if their businesses are to remain competitive. We strongly believe that employee empowerment and the energy that comes with feelings of ownership are necessary prerequisites for continuous improvement. Empower-

## WHAT DOES "EMPOWERING" MEAN?

*Power* means "control, authority, dominion." The prefix *em-* means "to put on to" or "to cover with." *Empowering*, then, is passing on authority and responsibility. As we refer to it here, empowerment occurs when power goes to employees who then experience a sense of ownership and control over their jobs.

Empowered individuals know that their jobs belong to them. Given a say in how things are done, employees feel more responsible. When they feel responsible, they show more initiative in their work, get more done, and enjoy the work more.

ment is facilitated by a combination of factors, including values, leadership actions, job structure, training, and reward systems, as illustrated in Figure 1.2.

An organization empowers its people when it enables employees to take on more responsibility and to make use of what they know and can learn. For some positions, there is no limit to the amount of empowerment that is possible through increases in job responsibilities. This is especially true in many professional and managerial positions. In such cases, the degree of empowerment is directly proportional to the amount of responsibility, as shown in Figure 1.3. Increasing responsibilities yield corresponding amounts of empowerment.

Unfortunately, this relationship does not apply to the wide range of single-task jobs designed for manufacturing and service organizations, such as clerks, process operators, and assemblers. Imagine Kathy, an operator on a glass bottle line, who for the past three years has been responsible for making sure the cooling line

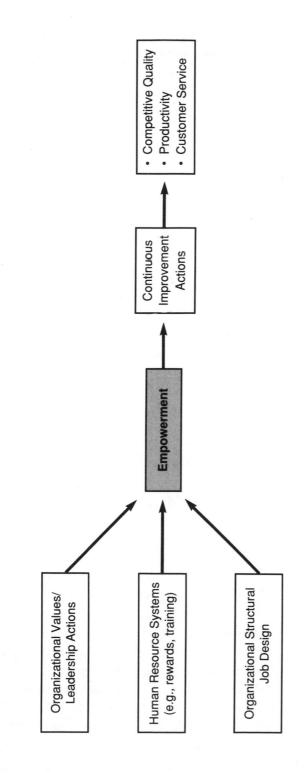

**Figure 1.2.** Empowerment in today's business environment.

runs smoothly on her shift. Her job is to keep the automated line from clogging and to let those on the hot side of the line know when the glass is not forming correctly. What responsibilities could be added to her job? She could be asked to maintain and even repair the equipment she operates. Perhaps she could take a more active role in quality inspection and improvement.

If the scope of Kathy's job continues to broaden, it will enhance her sense of empowerment and job ownership. At some point, however, the empowerment curve will begin to flatten out, because there is only so much she can do by *herself*. In other words, amounts of empowerment and responsibility eventually stop tracking in direct proportion to each other. Further duties would seem less meaningful, unrealistic, or too much like "make-work." They would no longer be feasible or desired. Figure 1.4 is probably a more accurate portrayal of the empowerment limits inherent in many individual job positions.

## Empowering Teams

How can you empower the individuals in your organization who are in low-ceiling jobs? One way to go beyond these limits is to begin thinking about the possibilities of empowering *groups* of workers. By giving several people collective responsibility for some meaningful output, you will have a better chance of opening up new possibilities for empowerment. Further, if the group is allowed to make decisions on its own—such as determining job assignments, scheduling vacations, and improving communication—even greater empowerment is possible. Figure 1.5 shows the impact of teams on empowerment and responsibility.

Teams are particularly effective in situations where it is impossible to greatly empower the individual alone. When a *group* takes on more job responsibilities and forms a team to share duties and

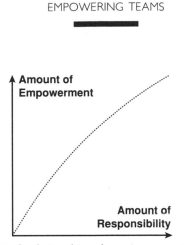

**Figure 1.3.** Theoretical relationship of empowerment and responsibility.

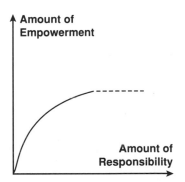

**Figure 1.4.** Limits of individual empowerment in most traditional jobs.

**Figure 1.5.** Impact of teams on empowerment and responsibility.

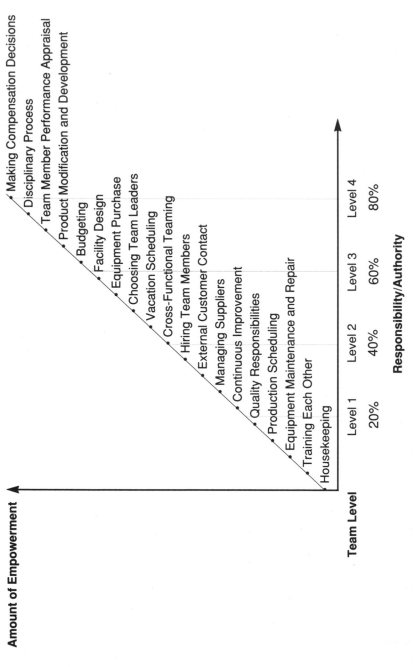

**Figure 1.6.** Team empowerment continuum.

achievements, new heights of employee empowerment are possible. The stretch of the curve at the upper right of Figure 1.5 represents the growth of a mature work team. *Zapp! The Lightning of Empowerment* (Byham, 1990) explains the relationship between empowerment and continuous improvement in more detail.

## GROWING EMPOWERED

Now let's take a closer look at the team's range of empowerment and how it changes over time. Figure 1.6, which shows the *team empowerment continuum*, converts "degree" of team responsibility to a four-point scale. This scale tracks the approximate percentage of responsibilities a team assumes, many of which were once reserved for leaders, managers, or support departments in more traditional organizations.

Level 1 on the scale represents the point at which a newly organized team begins. A team at level 1 is so new that it assumes little additional responsibility over its total process. In effect, a level-1 team is doing little more than what the individuals used to do on their own. Team members work together, but they have not yet assumed many of the responsibilities that still belong to their supervisor or others.

On the other end of the scale, at level 4, is a self-directed work team that has assumed perhaps 80 percent of the total possible job responsibilities, including a hefty portion of supervisory, managerial, and functional support group responsibilities. We say 80 percent because even in highly self-directed organizations, there are still people in leadership roles, although their total numbers and the nature of their jobs may have changed. A team at level 4 might be purchasing new equipment, hiring its own members, and making team bonus decisions—tasks their managers or human resource specialists once performed.

The team empowerment continuum in Figure 1.6 shows a partial list of common responsibilities and how they might be sequenced to empower a team. As teams progress over time, they assume not only a greater quantity of tasks but also more complex functions within tasks.

The responsibilities listed in the figure will be sequenced differently depending on the organization. Precise percentages are not easily calculated—in fact, the scale is more of a hypothetical model—but the idea is clear: Teams evolve by assuming higher-order responsibilities.

## SHIFTING RESPONSIBILITIES

Work teams grow more empowered as they increase ownership of their processes. Typically, that ownership grows from production activities (doing the job) to production control (coordinating the job) to leadership (group support and team governance). Chapter Two provides an in-depth look at the migration of responsibilities to teams.

Becoming a self-directed work team is an evolutionary process. Work teams don't spring up overnight. People adapt over time to greater degrees of responsibility, self-direction, and empowerment. However, an organization doesn't need to be at level 4 to reap the benefits of work teams. The empowerment continuum helps teams and management alike to understand where they are in terms of empowerment—and where they want to go. Chapter Two, "Moving Toward Empowered Teams: Rethinking Leadership Responsibilities," takes the continuum from the theoretical to the actual, describing in more detail the transition of responsibilities from management to the team. This shift is really what empowered teams are all about.

# MOVING TOWARD EMPOWERED TEAMS:
## Rethinking Leadership Responsibilities

No matter what your organizational structure is—teams or no teams, empowered or not—activities need to be planned, work assigned, and resources allocated. Every work setting calls for responsibilities such as setting goals, dealing with work habits or performance problems, solving operational problems, conducting meetings, communicating with other parts of the organization, coaching, certifying

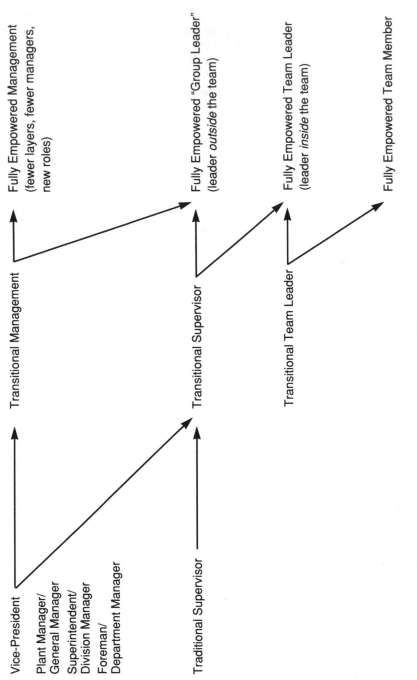

**Figure 2.1.** Transition of leadership/management responsibilities as teams emerge.

competency, and allocating compensation and rewards. For centuries the majority of these responsibilities have been delegated exclusively to organizational leaders.

## THE TRANSITION OF LEADERSHIP RESPONSIBILITIES

Leadership responsibilities don't disappear when self-directed work teams emerge. As Figure 2.1 shows, they are transferred over time. In general, the trend of redistribution is for leadership responsibilities to shift toward the team members themselves.

Shifts in responsibilities don't occur overnight. In fact, most organizations talk about a time span of two to five years to develop fully empowered teams. Some of these organizations specifically use the term "journey" to symbolize the process of taking a long trip—with some bumps along the way!

As leadership and managerial responsibilities shift to the team, the team becomes more empowered and self-directed. Often, more complex or difficult leadership responsibilities do not shift until the team has had a chance to get "up and running." A traditional management responsibility such as budgeting takes time to move down to the team member level.

The following examples illustrate some traditional management responsibilities that organizations have shifted to their teams:

- At Aid Association for Lutherans (AAL), teams do their own interviewing and make hiring decisions.

- At Cray Research, the supercomputer company, test results on new products are given directly to teams, which are responsible for solving and correcting problems on their own.

- At Colgate-Palmolive's plant in Ohio, teams design their own technical resource training manuals.

- At Semco S/A, a baking equipment manufacturing company in Brazil, team members decided where to locate a new plant.

- At Lake Superior Paper Industries, teams handle their own work scheduling, work assignments, and holiday and vacation planning.

- At Johnsonville Foods, a sausage company in Sheboygan, Wisconsin, whose sales skyrocketed from $4 million to $150 million as they embarked on an eight-year journey to self-direction, the company was presented with a lucrative opportunity to produce sausage for an outside company on a special basis. The managers were concerned that the large order would hurt current production schedules and affect quality. However, highly committed to empowerment, they let the teams decide whether to take the order. Team members decided to "go for it," scheduled the work, upheld quality standards, and gained an opportunity to learn how to handle larger volumes of work successfully.

- At West Virginia's Weirton Steel, a team was empowered to recommend a $5 million capital investment to renovate an aging mill that paid off in large profits, improved product quality and cost efficiency, and drastically reduced downtime.

- Our own company's printing operation has implemented teams successfully. These teams, as shown in the minutes of a bindery team meeting (Figure 2.2), are responsible for cross-training, continual improvement, and product quality.

As teams approach higher levels of empowerment, they begin to take on more of the responsibilities that are usually reserved

---

November 19,1990                                      2:30-3:30 p.m.

**Action Item Follow-ups:**

We received the electronic catalog. Dave C. and Bob F. are checking to see if the microswitches are in it.

We received the switches from Guckerts. They work on the Omni. The chargeable hour report for October was received. It is available to any bindery team members interested in reading it.

Bob F. is still trying to locate the Teflon spray for the tab laminator.

**Action Items:**

Dave C. will talk to Steve H. by 12-10-90 about ordering the laminator cutter.

Dave C. will talk to Mark B. by 12-10-90 about the EDS tabs. He will find out if the lamination is to be colored. Mylar will need to be ordered if special color is desired.

Bindery now has an in-basket. This will eliminate communication problems between daylight and afternoon shifts. It will also eliminate loss of literature given to the bindery by other teams.

Dave C. will talk to Patrice A. about making a sign for it by 12-10-90.

Dave C. and Bob F. will check the cutter in paper storage on 11-19-90 to see if it is straight and square.

Bob F. will talk to Kathy H. concerning a battery charger for the forklift by 11-26-90.

Bindery team members will start attending the press team meetings biweekly starting 12-7-90. This will help keep each team informed of problems they are having with each other's work. We will rotate our members so that each member has a chance to attend. The rotation list is as follows: Bob S., Dave C., Tom S., Bob F., Bob M., Melinda R., and Jerry B.

Bob S. started cross-training on the cutter on 11-19-90. He will be cross-trained for two weeks. He will then start further cross-training on the Omni.

Jerry B. started cross-training on the folder and further cross-trained on the Omni on 11-19-90. He will cross-train on the folder for two weeks. He will then cross-train on the cutter.

The bindery team will start testing to see if we can laminate wall charts without having any problems.

The team plan for biweekly maintenance will be started on the three-headed drill. The drill bits will be sharpened at this time.

The bindery team will start using the preprinted envelopes to send artwork to Bridgeville.

The test for the latest brochure will be undercut to assure proper fitting.

Some books were returned due to defects. Need to discuss with supplier.

Production reported that two boxes of materials were mislabeled. Need to determine possible reasons.

Team members are supposed to check the list on the wall by the tab cutter to see how many unlaminated tabs are to be cut for the service manual.

Dave C. will be on vacation until 12-3-90.

Congratulations to Melinda for completing the customer service seminar!

---

**Figure 2.2.**  Bindery team minutes at Development Dimensions International.

for management. Rethinking these responsibilities is the heart of making empowered teams more effective than traditional organizational structures.

## SHIFTING PROPORTIONS OF RESPONSIBILITY

While the redistribution of leadership responsibilities is what makes self-directed teams unique, organizations differ widely in terms of the degree to which these responsibilities are assumed by their teams.

Figures 2.3 and 2.4 present the Survey data regarding the distribution of leadership responsibilities of the organizations in our sample. The first of these figures relates to major production tasks, the second to management tasks.

At the left end of the scale is the percentage of respondents who indicated that a task was still retained primarily by a "formal" leader outside the team. At the right end of the scale is the percentage of respondents who indicated that a task was predominantly the responsibility of the team. The center area shows the percentage of respondents who indicated that the task was shared by the team and its leaders.

As you can see, the majority of tasks are shared between the team and first-line leaders outside the team. This finding deserves interpretation since the very term "self-direction" may conjure up images of an organization without leadership. We conclude that one reason for the high proportion of shared tasks is that the great majority of organizations making the transition to empowered work teams truly believe in a shared leadership model. Although many responsibilities are shifted to the team, there still may be a need for some degree of first- and second-level leadership. The majority of organizations reporting that they use self-directed teams still have supervisors and managers in place (although different titles may be used). While there is a wealth of data on the positive impact of empowerment and teams, we are unaware of research that directly relates the *degree* to which leaders transfer their "traditional" responsibilities to organizational effectiveness. In fact, it may be that a term like "shared leadership teams" more accurately reflects reality than does "self-directed teams."

A second reason for the high number of shared tasks is that the majority of teams in the Survey were less than two years old, and leadership transfer, as we mentioned, occurs gradually as the team matures. We suspect that if we surveyed these organizations again in two years, the percentages would have moved toward greater team control.

## DEFINING LEADERSHIP WITHIN THE TEAM

In Chapter Seven we will deal in greater depth with the changing role of the leader. However, it is helpful at this point to consider several ways the leadership role is handled within the team structure. Reviewing these models will provide some perspective for the rest of the book.

Most organizations that implement self-directed teams still maintain some sort of within-the-team leader, often called the *team leader* or *team coordinator*. Usually the team leader is not a member of management but is, in fact, a team member who is willing and able to take on some of the coordination functions for the team. Typically, a team leader still spends time actually performing various production or service tasks but also helps the team accomplish its leadership responsibilities. Often the team leader serves

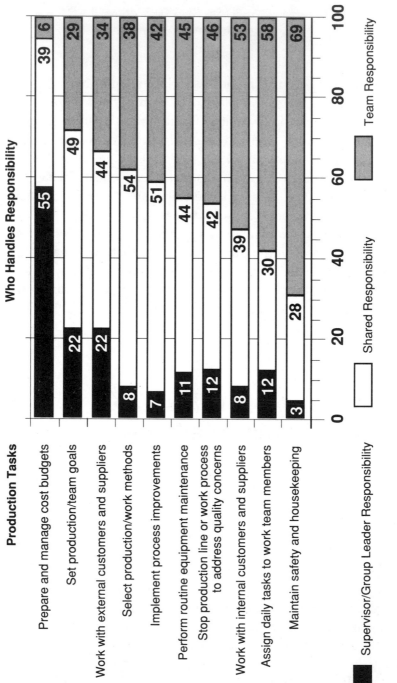

**Figure 2.3.** Percentage of production tasks assumed by teams. Data extracted from Wellins, Wilson, Katz, Laughlin, and Day, 1990.

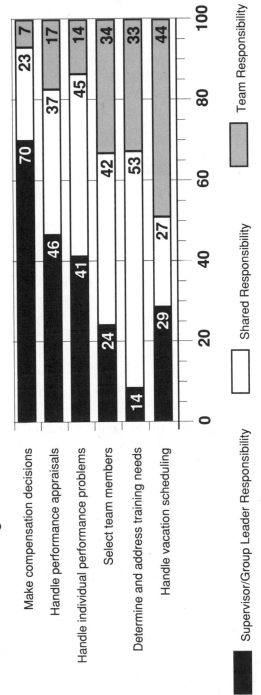

**Management Tasks**

**Who Handles Responsibility**

| Task | Supervisor/Group Leader | Shared | Team |
|---|---|---|---|
| Make compensation decisions | 70 | 23 | 7 |
| Handle performance appraisals | 46 | 37 | 17 |
| Handle individual performance problems | 41 | 45 | 14 |
| Select team members | 24 | 42 | 34 |
| Determine and address training needs | 14 | 53 | 33 |
| Handle vacation scheduling | 29 | 27 | 44 |

■ Supervisor/Group Leader Responsibility

☐ Shared Responsibility

▨ Team Responsibility

**Figure 2.4.** Percentage of management tasks assumed by teams. Data extracted from Wellins, Wilson, Katz, Laughlin, and Day, 1990.

as a spokesperson for the team, coordinates team activities with other departments or teams, and devotes time to training new team members. However, in other organizations the team leader may play only the role of "internal facilitator," helping the team decide how various leadership responsibilities will be divided among team members. In many cases, the position of team leader is permanent; in others, all team members have an opportunity to rotate into the position on a four- to six-month basis.

There is usually, but not always, a leader outside the team, often called the *group leader* (which is by no means a universal term). This layer of leadership combines some of the responsibilities assumed by traditional first-level supervisors with those of middle managers. Leaders at this level usually have large spans of control, sometimes ranging over 100 team members. For example, AT&T Operator Services in Richmond, Virginia, moved from a span of control of one leader for each twelve members to one leader for each seventy-two members. As teams mature, it is not uncommon for six or more teams to report to a single group leader.

Group leaders frequently play a coordinating and facilitating role. They help teams communicate with one another and serve as a conduit for information that flows from the teams to other organizational departments and from these departments back to the teams. Figure 2.5 shows a typical day in the life of a group leader.

## FEWER MANAGERS—FEWER PEOPLE?

Sixty-eight percent of the organizations in the Survey reported that eventually they were able to run their team-based organizations with fewer managers. Ninety-five percent of those who operated their teams with fewer managers found the change to be beneficial. This strong response is worth noting. It appears that the large

| | |
|---|---|
| 6:30 | *Meet with third-shift group/team leaders to review schedules/issues* |
| 6:45 | *Meet with team leaders—review department performance, provide feedback* |
| 7 | *Coach team leader on performance problems she is confronting with a new* |
| 7:15 | *team member* |
| 7:30 | |
| 7:45 | *Fill in for team member attending safety committee meeting* |
| **8** | |
| 8:15 | |
| 8:30 | ▼ |
| 8:45 | |
| **9** | *Facilitate an interteam meeting about a new production process* |
| 9:15 | |
| 9:30 | |
| 9:45 | |
| **10** | |
| 10:15 | ▼ |
| 10:30 | |
| 10:45 | |
| **11** | *Lunch* |
| 11:15 | ▼ |
| 11:30 | *Facilitate training program on team meeting skills* |
| 11:45 | |
| **12** | |
| 12:15 | |
| 12:30 | |
| 12:45 | ▼ |
| **1** | *Attend group leader meeting* |
| 1:15 | ▼ |
| 1:30 | *Prepare for appraisal with team leader* |
| 1:45 | *Conduct appraisal with team leader* |
| **2** | |
| 2:15 | ▼ |
| 2:30 | *Conduct new supplier committee meeting* |
| 2:45 | ▼ |
| **3** | *Facilitate intergroup quality action team (special assignment)* |
| 3:15 | ▼ |
| 3:30 | *Meet with swing-shift team leaders* |
| 3:45 | ▼ |
| **4** | |
| *Other responsibilities:* | *Help member prepare for a presentation    Meet with staff team*  *Help member learn a task    Conduct training program* |

**Figure 2.5.**  A day in the life of a group leader.

number of managers and the multiple layers of supervision inherent in our business culture have interfered with our ability to compete.

However, these data do not necessarily indicate that self-directed work teams require fewer people in the organization; an organization might need fewer supervisors and managers but more team members. A common mistake in planning the creation of teams is to assume that the teams can take on many of their supervisors' responsibilities while maintaining the same work load as before.

For example, Hannaford Brothers Co., a grocery chain that uses teams in its warehouse operation, reports that team members who share a variety of leadership responsibilities can end up devoting more than 20 percent of their time to these activities. Thus, the company had to make sure that the teams were adequately staffed to handle all the day-to-day work.

Although it is true that eventually fewer managers and supervisors are required in self-directed organizations, the move toward fewer leadership layers and positions does not have to be accompanied by massive layoffs. Managers and first-line leaders can be offered jobs as trainers, team facilitators, and technical experts.

A large aerospace company in Canada decided to reduce the number of middle management positions by 50 percent. The middle managers whose jobs had been eliminated were reassigned to the new organization as either facilitators or technical experts. With the new organizational structure firmly in place, the facilitators had a goal to help make that structure work. As teams became more self-reliant, the facilitators were given new job responsibilities.

Similarly, a large chemical company formed a committee of managers to design new value-added positions that would use their skills and knowledge. Several important coordinating positions were created, which provided an incentive for managers to relinquish their traditional roles.

Rethinking responsibilities means a shift in power, and such a shift can be very difficult for both those who lose power and those who assume it. Contrary to popular belief, the role of leaders in self-directed organizations is far from obsolete. However, the role is rapidly changing and evolving, as we will see in Chapter Seven.

# CONFRONTING NEW ORGANIZATIONAL QUESTIONS:
## How Teams Function in a Redesigned Organization

The trouble with trying to describe how work teams operate is that there is no such thing as a "typical" team. Different organizations give birth to teams of various sorts, and teams within an organization may be at different points on the empowerment continuum at any given time. Nevertheless, this chapter will give you a better understanding of the mechanics of work teams. It is based on questions we have been asked by companies that are interested in starting teams. The answers come from a combination of individual and group interviews, the Survey we conducted jointly with *Industry Week* and the Association for Quality and Participation, and our own experience with self-directed teams.

## "What percentage of your work force is currently organized into self-directed work teams?"

SELF-DIRECTED TEAMS are used by a substantial number of organizations—26 percent, according to the Survey estimate. This figure was recently corroborated in an independent study of 845 line managers conducted by Wyatt Corporation, a professional survey firm. Twenty-seven percent of the sample reported using self-managed teams (Moskal, 1991). Yet, in the organizations that are using teams, only a small portion of the work force is actually functioning in teams. The Survey data show that 59 percent of the organizations that report using teams have less than 10 percent of their current work force organized into teams. Edward Lawler, who has studied high-involvement management extensively, recently told participants at the 1990 International Conference on Self-Managed Work Teams that by his estimate, self-directed work team members comprise less than 2 percent of the total U.S. work force.

Of the organizations we surveyed that have implemented work teams, the majority—82 percent—phased them into existing operations. Eighteen percent started as part of a new or ''greenfield'' operation.

Close to 80 percent of all organizations involved in the Survey come from the manufacturing sector. Manufacturing operations have pioneered the team concept and are experiencing rapid growth of self-directed teams. At the same time, many white-collar organizations now use self-directed work teams. These include Aid Association for Lutherans (AAL); AT&T Credit Corporation; Monogram Credit Corporation; Shenandoah Life Insurance Company; the St. Paul Companies; and IDS Financial Services, a division of American Express.

---

## "What titles are used for people in work teams?"

WHILE TITLES ARE NOT IMPORTANT per se, they do symbolize the changes inherent in the move toward self-direction. Increasing numbers of organizations, especially those that incorporate high employee involvement, are moving away from terms such as "subordinate" and "employee" and are using more participative titles. For example, "team member" is used at Toyota Automotive in Lexington, Kentucky, and at Lake Superior Paper Industries in Duluth, Minnesota. Subaru-Isuzu Automotive and Semco in Brazil use "associate." The Tennessee Eastman division of Eastman Kodak Company changed from "operator" to "technician" when it instituted work teams.

We have also heard terminology like "team representative" and "customer satisfaction associate" (the latter at a white-collar organization). A Steelcase associate recently showed us his business card with the job title "World Class Manufacturer." These titles are not different for the sake of difference; they are symbols representing major changes in function and responsibility.

In most cases, the title "supervisor" changes to "group leader," "coordinator," "communicator," "coach," or "facilitator." One organization refers to its first-line leaders as "unleaders."

## "What is the ideal size of a work team?"

THE SURVEY INDICATES that the average size of a work team ranges from six to twelve people. Size is dictated by two principles. First, many organizations moving to the team concept go through a work design process (see Chapter Six). This process helps to determine which positions and functions logically belong together. Second, it is better to keep your teams on the smaller side. Research in industrial and social psychology indicates that too many participants can hinder the group process (Hackman, 1987; Gladstein, 1984).

Monogram Credit Corporation, which implemented self-directed work teams in its white-collar environment, has ten to twelve people on a team. Schreiber Foods, a large cheese processor in Tempe, Arizona, has about seven people per team. General Electric's aircraft engine plant in Rutland, Vermont, has twelve to fourteen people on each team.

## "When and how often should teams meet?"

ALMOST ALL FACILITIES employing work teams provide opportunities for members to meet on the job. Teams may hold brief communication meetings at the beginning of shifts and longer meetings (two to three hours) once or twice a month to discuss specific team issues surrounding communication, discipline, equipment, and quality. At General Electric, team members meet for twenty minutes to an hour—either once a week or twice a month—to share information and to work on improvements. The team holds longer meetings to deal with special situations. Monogram Credit Corporation holds five-minute meetings every morning in addition to weekly, one-hour team sessions for problem solving.

In addition to team sessions, members often represent their teams in cross-team meetings on a variety of issues such as quality, training, start-up, and safety. In all cases, team members are paid for the time spent in these meetings.

Those who are considering teams for the first time (especially line managers) often ask how work gets done around so many meetings. On the whole, meetings help productivity rather than hinder it. It is important to trust the team because team members can determine the necessary balance between meeting time and production time.

---

## "What, and how common, is multiskilling?"

ONE OF THE HALLMARKS of self-directed teams is that they embrace the concepts of *multiskilling* and *job rotation*. These terms are relatively simple to understand, but they are not always easy to execute, especially when they are tied to reward systems. In many traditional organizations, employees are assigned a single, narrow job and may end up performing the same tasks forever.

Often, in team environments, members are expected to learn every job on the team and, in some cases, to go on to learn jobs on other teams as well. This concept has two obvious advantages. First, it gives organizations the flexibility to handle shifting requirements and cover for absent team members. Second, most team members see the change as positive because the variety provides greater job challenges and better understanding of the total process.

There are many positive examples of multiskilling. At the newer team-based automotive plants such as the Toyota plant in Georgetown, Kentucky, the Subaru-Isuzu plant in Lafayette, Indiana, and General Motors' Saturn plant in Spring Hill, Tennessee, every team member learns all the assembly tasks for which the team is responsible. At GE Rutland, work team members are grouped around products. They learn all the processes necessary to manufacture their products, including basic skills, casting, milling, and broaching.

Job rotation and multiskilling are not limited to blue-collar organizations. As we mentioned, AAL team members can learn as many as twenty different service-related jobs necessary to meet the needs of their customers. There was a time when AAL used an assembly line method in which individuals performed specific tasks. But times have changed.

Similarly, at IDS Financial Services, team members who were once responsible for single, narrow, functional tasks now handle a variety of jobs, including establishing business accounts, performing changes in account ownership, and redeeming mutual fund shares.

Respondents in the Survey reported that they use multiskilling as follows:

| Degree of Use | Survey Respondents (%) |
| --- | --- |
| To a great extent | 21 |
| To some extent | 42 |
| To a limited extent | 25 |
| Not at all | 12 |

One bit of advice: Be careful of mandating universal multiskill systems in situations where some jobs require complex job skills. It can be very time consuming and costly to train everyone in high-skill jobs and, once trained, they may not get enough practice time to maintain their skills. We know of several manufacturing organizations that exempted a few jobs from their multiskill plans, most notably because certain jobs required years of training and technical expertise. In such cases, it may be best to leave some specialists out of the multiskill plan.

---

## "How do you position various support activities such as maintenance?"

AS ORGANIZATIONS MOVE toward self-direction, support functions such as training, finance, maintenance, and quality control often undergo a transformation as well. There are a number of methods organizations can use to integrate support functions into the team process.

Many organizations still have traditional support departments where special attempts must be made to change the focus from "the team serves us" to "we serve the team." Positions in finance, accounting, and administration are a good example. In traditional organizations, these jobs were designed to control expenses, budgets, and purchases. While control is still important, the nature of these jobs changes with a move to empowered teams. In one manufacturing organization, associates in the financial unit regularly ask each team what types of accounting systems they need in order to be effective; then they proceed to help the teams develop these systems. They also offer the teams training with regard to budgeting and understanding the plant's accounting system.

Sometimes an organization maintains separate support departments but establishes formal liaisons between the work teams and these departments. In such cases, teams may appoint one member to be a "maintenance coordinator"; another a "safety coordinator"; a third, a "training coordinator"; and so on. When necessary, these coordinators seek out the functional experts and take their skills and knowledge back to the work team.

A third option is to integrate support functions into the work team. In these situations, either the team members learn support functions or an outside expert in the function becomes part of the team. An example would be inclusion of a maintenance expert in a team. The separate maintenance department then ceases to exist in the organization, or it is greatly reduced because the work team performs most maintenance functions.

Divisions within IBM and Tennessee Eastman have adopted this third option. GE Rutland is moving in this direction by bringing some maintenance and engineering functions into its work teams. Similarly, Pfizer International, headquartered in New York, formed white-collar teams and incorporated within these teams many of the functions required for a product launch, including medical research, patent registration, and marketing.

Training is another job that many teams have begun to assume. Team leaders and team members handle both technical training and other training in areas such as meeting skills and group dynamics. In these instances, the human resource staff members function as facilitators and resource experts instead of assuming responsibility for all direct training.

It is interesting to note that, in some cases, support departments are organizing into their own self-directed teams and are implementing plans for multiskilling. In manufacturing operations, it is common for maintenance departments to form themselves into cross-skilled teams. This is true in most new North American Japanese automotive plant start-up situations such as Toyota in Georgetown, Kentucky; Subaru-Isuzu in Lafayette, Indiana; and CAMI Automotive, a joint venture of General Motors of Canada and Japan's Suzuki Motor Company. Associates in these teams are expected to acquire a full range of maintenance skills, including electrical, welding, and pneumatics.

In a handful of manufacturing companies, white-collar associates in support departments are also forming their own self-directed teams. For example, both Corning and Texas Instruments are experimenting with self-directed management information system teams. Du Pont has organized personnel in its computer systems department into teams that are assigned to specific areas of the company's extensive research operation.

## "How do your teams handle their shift transfer responsibilities?"

IN TEAM-ORIENTED manufacturing organizations, shift transfers are dealt with in the same way they are in more traditional organizations—through effective communication between shifts. Often the team leader or coordinator stays late or comes in early to discuss problems and opportunities.

Many organizations have chosen to delegate the role of shift communication to the team itself. Schreiber Foods uses a system that calls for "communicators" on each team to take on an inter-team communication role. In addition, team members may meet with members of the next shift informally, as needed, during the shift transfer. Occasionally teams get together for more formal meetings to discuss common problems.

In some cases, the problem is eliminated by forming teams that cross shift boundaries. Becton, Dickinson and Company has adopted this approach with a team that is completely responsible for producing a product across all three shifts. The team members decide how to arrange shift coordination and schedule production. For instance, in order to make more time for meetings during the week, team members may choose to work overtime on Saturday to build up their inventories.

Shift coordination is not as simple a problem to solve as it might seem. One company we worked with has a plant that makes molds for aircraft engine parts. One team member on the third shift decided to move a piece of equipment to another location to reduce her "time in motion." Unfortunately, the team member, who was new, was performing her work out of sequence. For her, the equipment move was helpful; for others, performing according to sequence, it was a mess. The leader of the first shift got angry and complained to management. The second-shift team thought it was some sort of experiment and made no comment. It took two days to straighten things out. The problem is now avoided through better communication and having someone accountable for shift transfer coordination.

## "What responsibilities do team members have outside their team?"

IN MANY ORGANIZATIONS, involvement extends beyond the intact work team. Teams may be asked to play a role in choosing training programs, developing safety policies and procedures, handling disciplinary appeals, developing skill-based pay scales, or preparing annual business plans. These organization-wide issues affect *all* teams. Team members also may serve on company-wide quality action teams or quality circles to deal with specific quality problems that affect several teams.

What often happens, as shown in Figure 3.1, is that members of self-directed teams serve on organization-wide teams to help decide company policy and processes for specific areas. These assignments are periodically rotated among team members. Figure 3.1 shows a model used by one company. Each team designates a team member to serve on an organization-wide team or task force in an area like budgeting or training. Members on these special teams usually are responsible for keeping the members of their regular work teams informed about their progress and gathering their input.

## "What relationship do team members have with customers and suppliers?"

THE SURVEY INDICATES that many team members have responsibility for communicating with customers and sup-

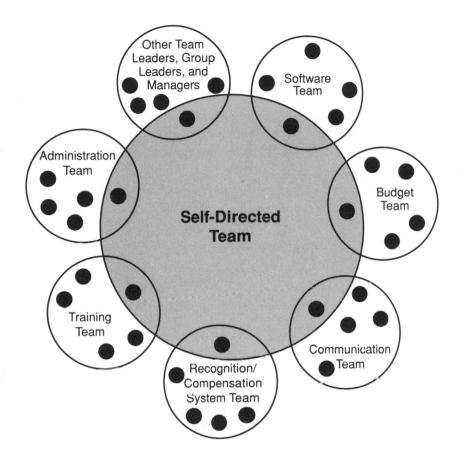

**Figure 3.1.** Job assignments within a team.

pliers. Organizations today tend to think in terms of *internal* and *external* suppliers and customers. This concept links naturally with Just-In-Time "pull" systems, where each team accepts or "pulls" partially assembled products or supplies from another team only if they meet accepted standards.

This approach requires constant communication among teams, which leads to improved quality and productivity. Before teams were installed in one organization, a systems analyst with

questions about a specification had to go to her boss, who in turn
went to *her* boss, who then went to the department that supplied
the specification. There, the query went down two levels to the
person who wrote the original specification. Communication was
often interrupted or broken down, and in most cases it took a
lot of time. Once the organization had developed empowered
teams, all team members dealt directly with their internal customers. There were significant improvements immediately: The
analyst could call her internal customer directly, and questions
that once took a day to answer now took only a few minutes.

Similarly, more teams are dealing directly with their external customers and suppliers. In some organizations, team members visit external customers to learn about their needs and to
help solve problems. Team members also can be called upon to
help (and train) their external vendors to do a better job in meeting the team's quality requirements. One GE plant chartered a
plane and sent a large group of engineers, managers, and team
members on a one-day visit to one of its biggest clients—the U.S.
Navy. This day of talking with, and listening to, such an important client proved to be an invaluable experience. At Johnsonville Foods, customer letters are forwarded to line workers who
decide how to respond to complaints.

As Figure 2.3 showed, 53 percent of the Survey respondents
indicated that their team plays the major role in dealing with
*internal* customers and suppliers. Thirty-four percent indicated that
the team plays the major role in dealing with *external* customers
and suppliers.

---

## "What is the role of teams in selecting new team members?"

MANY TEAM-BASED ORGANIZATIONS have reached
the stage where team members participate in the selection of new

team members. Frequently, one or two team representatives are given the assignment of working with the organization's personnel department to conduct an initial screening of candidates; however, the whole team participates in the final decision. To help team members make sound (and legally defensible) decisions, it is common to provide interview skills training.

## "What role does the team play in appraising its own members?"

IN MOST ORGANIZATIONS, the team itself does not assume the major role in appraising team performance. Forty-six percent of the organizations in the Survey indicated that leaders outside the team handle appraisals; 17 percent said that the responsibility is shared; and 37 percent responded that the team takes the lead in appraising performance. Based on these results, it appears that appraisal is a responsibility that is difficult for teams to accept (and perhaps for management to give up).

This is understandable. It can be difficult for teammates who work closely together to be critical of each other, even in a constructive manner. As one manager put it, ''Team members are fine at giving positive feedback to one another, but negative or constructive feedback—forget it!'' Appraisals often are tied to compensation, which makes it even more difficult for team members to become involved in the process.

While leaders outside the team still conduct most formal appraisals, many organizations are establishing methods for collecting peer comments from team members. These data are then incorporated into the appraisal process.

While it is certainly not the norm, some self-directed organizations with more mature teams, such as TRW, have implemented full peer appraisal systems. Obviously, such systems require carefully designed processes and training. They are far more difficult to implement than normal "top-down" appraisal systems. Skills such as setting goals, providing feedback, and conducting performance ratings must be taught to the whole team. In addition, taking the appraisal out of the one-on-one context and putting it in a group context can make interpersonal dynamics very complex.

## "What role does the team play in improving performance and disciplining its own team members?"

FORTY-FIVE PERCENT of the organizations in the Survey reported that their teams play a role in handling problems involving team members' performance. An interesting example of "team wisdom" comes from a large chemical company, where the team handled a situation in which a work team member violated a safety procedure. The team asked the offending member to produce a videotape depicting the safety hazard in question and showing what had been done to correct it. He was asked to use this tape to train all the plant's teams on the correct safety procedure. Everyone learned and justice was served. In fact, the team member actually enjoyed the training opportunity.

Lake Superior Paper Industries lets its teams handle a performance or work habit problem through a process of progressive discipline. The first step involves a feedback discussion between the offending team member and the rest of the team. If the offender does not act to correct the problem, the second step involves writing up a social contract that demonstrates the team member's commitment to take corrective action. The offending team member signs the contract, as do the other members of the team. If the performance or work habit problem persists, the third step is for the team to suggest that the offender take a day off without pay to reflect on whether he or she wants to continue to work at the mill. If there is still no change, there is a fourth step: a second written contract, this time with a specific warning date when the offending team member *must* have corrected the performance or work habit problem. As a final step, the team has the right to terminate the member based on continued poor performance or work habits.

Terminated team members who feel that they have been treated unfairly can appeal the decision by presenting their grievances to a special panel. This panel consists of the president of Lake Superior Paper Industries and four peers from the team, one of whom is chosen by the aggrieved team member. This panel has the power to overturn the team's decision. At last report, two terminated employees at Lake Superior had appealed the decision; both terminations were upheld by the special panel.

Subaru-Isuzu and other organizations use a similar disciplinary process. Team members who serve on the grievance panel receive special training in evaluating evidence and communicating decisions in order to enhance the fairness of the decision-making process.

## "Do teams have any sort of special compensation or reward system?"

THERE ARE THREE MAJOR FORMS of compensation for team members: base pay, skill-based pay, and some sort of bonus plan such as gain sharing.

The compensation scheme that receives the most attention is skill-based pay, because it ties so closely with multiskilling. Ledford (1989) describes three "dimensions" of skills that can be rewarded in skill-based systems. The first is *depth:* knowing a lot about a specific area. For example, a team member might first need to know how to operate a piece of equipment; then move on to learn basic maintenance for that piece of equipment; and eventually operate, maintain, and repair the equipment. The second skill dimension is *breadth*. Here, team members learn all the jobs on the team and may eventually learn jobs on other teams as well. Third, there can be a *vertical* skill dimension that includes leadership skills, such as training, safety, and leading meetings, that are necessary across all jobs on the team.

To set up a skill-based system, common job skills are organized into "blocks." As each new block of skills is acquired, team members receive an increase in base pay. Hundreds of organizations now use skill-based pay for their teams, including Weyerhaeuser Company, Tennessee Eastman, the Boeing Company, Whirlpool Corporation, and Square D Company.

Pay-for-skill systems are not without problems, though. First, they are difficult to formulate and deliver. Organizations with this type of system must use a testing or certification process to ensure that team members actually have acquired the new skills. Certification processes include a combination of on-the-job performance tests, written paper-and-pencil tests, and oral exams. Both leaders and fellow team members are involved in certifying team members.

Second, training is a key issue. Team members need extensive instruction and instructional materials to master new skills. Often this can mean developing an extensive curriculum, including the acquisition of volumes of technical manuals. At the Colgate-Palmolive plant in Ohio, the teams themselves participated in developing these materials.

Third, several organizations with pay-for-skill systems report that although team members are learning the new skills in order to get higher pay, they don't use the skills and eventually lose proficiency. As a result, some organizations have shifted to "pay-for-use" or "pay-for-performance" plans. The idea is excellent, although in many jobs it can be difficult to measure the application of skills.

Still another concern is affordability. Not every organization needs—or can afford to have—every team member capable of performing every task. Along this line, AAL has come up with a unique solution. It assigns payroll budgets to teams during each business year. Each team decides how to distribute the budget within its pay-for-skill system.

On the whole, reactions to skill-based systems have been positive, probably because these systems directly reinforce the concept of job rotation and multiskilling, which in turn allows organizations to increase their flexibility and improve quality and productivity.

Another type of compensation that is becoming more common with self-directed work teams is a form of gain sharing or profit sharing. With these systems, team members receive some sort of compensation for gains in performance over an established baseline. There are a variety of gain- and profit-sharing plans, of which division or unit profit sharing is the most common. A few systems are based on the performance of a single team or group. One important benefit of this concept, particularly from a team perspective, is that it rewards *group* rather than *individual* performance (assuming that the bonus is paid equally to all team members). In establishing such a plan, it is critical to have measurement systems in place as well as a reliable baseline of performance against which to measure improvements. Usually it is best to implement these systems a year or two after the move to self-direction, especially in new plant start-ups.

In addition to formal compensation, many organizations implement other total team reward and recognition systems, including quality and safety awards. These awards usually take the form of certificates, trophies, small cash bonuses, or some sort of motivational event. The Toyota plant in Georgetown, Kentucky, has instituted a program called "Personal Touch," in which each work team receives a budget to spend on team motivation and reward activities.

The general types of compensation systems used by the Survey respondents are shown here according to the percentages of companies employing them. Note that some companies use more than one type of system.

| Type of Compensation System | Use by Survey Respondents (%) |
|---|---|
| Individual merit increases | 59 |
| Individual gain sharing | 10 |
| Bonuses for productivity | 12 |
| Pay for skills or knowledge | 38 |

## "How does a team handle a member's transfer from one team to another?"

OCCASIONALLY THERE WILL BE a vacancy on a team, and a member of another team will want to fill it. Perhaps this person senses a better fit on the new team or sees an opportunity to acquire new skills that might increase his or her compensation or knowledge levels. In general, team members are free to apply for positions on other teams.

Many organizations view a team transfer as seriously as a new hire or any other selection decision. The team with the vacancy usually is responsible for filling the position and handles most of the steps in the internal applicant's selection process.

# "What are the basic dimensions required by team members?"

IN CONNECTION WITH the development of selection and training programs, we have conducted more than 100 job analyses of team member positions in empowered organizations. Table 3.1 shows the typical dimensions that are considered important for a highly empowered team member.

**TABLE 3.1**
**Critical Team Member Dimensions**

| Dimension | Importance to Teams |
|---|---|
| Ability to Learn (Applied Learning) | Multiskilling/job rotation |
| Analysis (Problem Identification) | Team solves its own problems |
| Attention to Detail | Focus on continuous improvement |
| Influence | Persuades others inside and outside the organization |
| Initiative | Emphasis on continual improvement |
| Job Fit (Motivation to Work in an Empowered Setting) | Job satisfaction, reduction of turnover, team "owns" decisions |
| Judgment (Problem Solution) | Quality/productivity/team issues |
| Oral Communication | Presents ideas to others |
| Planning and Organizing (Work Management) | Team determines work/production scheduling |
| Teamwork (Cooperation) | Team members work with others on their own work team and on other teams |
| Technical/Professional Proficiency | Job rotation/multiskilling |
| Tolerance for Stress | Handles ambiguity/stress related to new demands and roles |
| Training and Coaching | Team members teach and train each other |
| Work Standards | Quality/productivity focus |

The job analysis that produces lists like these also provides a detailed definition of each dimension and specific examples of behavior, motivations, or knowledge that illustrate each dimension (see Chapter Eight). As teams progress along the empowerment continuum, and as their members take on more responsibilities, the *weighting* of the dimensions changes, but there is little change in the *actual* dimensions.

## "What role does the union play in self-directed teams?"

SURPRISINGLY, 53 PERCENT of the Survey respondents implemented teams in facilities that were represented by unions. Unions can and do play an active role in team implementation. Survey respondents indicated substantial union involvement with self-directed teams (SDTs), as shown in the following list:

| Type of Union Involvement | Survey Respondents (%) |
|---|---|
| The union initiated SDTs in the organization. | 3 |
| The union actively participated in the design of SDTs. | 21 |
| Union members participated in SDTs in the organization. | 49 |
| The union was against SDTs in the organization. | 6 |
| The union adopted a neutral position. | 21 |

A new Hershey Foods Corporation plant in Pennsylvania; I/N Tek (a joint venture between Inland Steel Industries and Nippon Steel) in Indiana; A. O. Smith Automotive Works in Milwaukee, Wisconsin; and the Buick City plant of General Motors in Flint, Michigan, are all excellent examples of organizations that have worked cooperatively with unions in moving toward self-direction. While teams have at times created controversy within union ranks, especially at the national level, there is general agreement that the concept can work successfully in unionized companies (Robenstein, 1989). Empowerment can benefit both parties. We have briefed several unions on the team concept prior to implementation, and the response has been very positive.

One overriding principle is that unions should be involved from the beginning. Self-direction (and empowerment in general) must be done *with* the union, not *to* the union. This involvement is not limited to educating the union on the team concept; it also means including union representatives in site visits, having them serve on both steering committees and design teams, and providing them with the skills and training they need to make the transition. At A. O. Smith, the idea to move to teams came from the union itself (Hoerr, 1989a).

One other point to keep in mind. It is probably best to implement self-direction when there is some reasonable assurance of employment stability. We know of one organization that started teams and one year later experienced a significant layoff—with devastating consequences. Occurrences like this not only hurt the team concept; they may set the entire workplace culture back to the Dark Ages.

# A Day in the Life
# of a Self-Directed Team:
## A Case Study

Schreiber Foods' R. G. Bush plant is producing over twice as much quality product as a traditional cheese factory the same size. Schreiber's highly efficient cheese-making machine, with a footprint of only approximately 4,000 square feet, turns about six million pounds of milk a week into more than a million pounds of cheese. There's a great flow inside RGB's walls as a result of computer-operated control systems and self-directed teams.

Schreiber is now the second-largest cheese manufacturer in the United States, next to Kraft. The fifty-three people at the Tempe, Arizona, location (out of a total of 2,300 employees) make bulk cheese for other Schreiber plants that further process and package the cheese under private labels or sell it to the largest national fast food chains.

It's 6 A.M. Monday at the plant. The Green team—six associates in hairnets—comes in to relieve six workers on the Silver team, who have just put in a long night. Each team works a twelve-hour shift, seven times every fourteen days. There is little ceremony in the shift change, and there are no supervisors.

Gerald, the "communicator" from the Silver team, tells Ed, Green's communicator, about a potential pH problem in the system. The two men walk toward the conference room discussing the situation.

Meanwhile, Bobby and Tim are assuming their positions in the glass "process control room" high above the operation, taking over two upholstered chairs from the people they're relieving. The "PC room" looks a little like the control center of a nuclear plant or space center. There is a long console with four computer terminals in the center of the room facing a wall paneled in switches, meters, and recorders. Large, colorful computer screens display representations of all portions of the plant's process, all the parameters, and as many buttons as a compulsive controller could possibly want. This is a very powerful and complex remote control. With his fingers on the keyboard, Tim says, "No one else makes cheese like we do." (Figure 4.1 shows the layout of Schreiber's facility.)

Tim is checking his back-end computer screen as the team member he replaces warns him about the condition of the pH in the system. Each team uses large handwritten master logs—forms that team members designed themselves—to keep track of its run performance. The pH is at its lowest allowable limit, and everything else is normal. "Watch the second evaporator," he says.

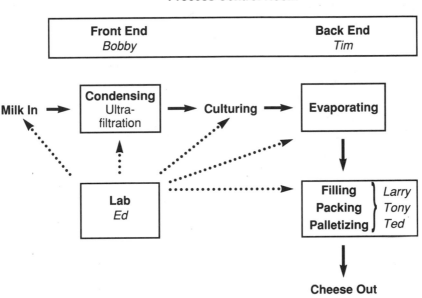

**Figure 4.1.**  Schreiber Foods' RGB cheese-processing operation. Courtesy of Schreiber Foods.

"It's going to need a CIP [cleaning in place] soon." "No problem," says Tim.

Bobby, who is in charge of the front end today, is finding out from the person he is relieving which silos are standardized and which are available to run. He learns that one is scheduled to have its agitator replaced during his shift, and he is reminded that a UF (ultra-filtration) cleaning is due.

The remaining three Green team members—Larry, Tony, and Ted—are settling in at their stations down on the floor in the barrel room area. Larry has the highest technical ratings, so it's interesting to see him rolling up his sleeves for a day of manual labor. He would rather be in the PC room explaining the process to visitors, but he talks instead about the importance of control as he pushes around the heavy barrels: "Seeing that all we do is make cheese, this plant is highly technical. One screwup can cost millions. A little inattentiveness on the back end, for instance, and you could have a rotor-to-wall contact that would just trash that rotor. It would take six to eight months to replace it. That means our production would be cut in half for six months. Wouldn't take much to screw it up."

Larry, Tony, and Ted will spend their entire shift making cardboard barrels, filling each with 500 pounds of cheese, and palletizing them. They prefer rotating jobs every few hours. They estimate that they will probably package about a hundred barrels today, about 50,000 pounds total. Cheese making is still a delicate process, so output is hard to control fully. Anything can happen in a day.

The RGB plant has seven eleven-person teams: four production teams (Green, Silver, Red, and Blue), one eleven-person maintenance team, one support team (with specialties such as culturing and sanitizing), and a small management team.

Ed and Gerald, the two communicators, are still in the conference room. They have been joined by Scott, the manager of quality improvement, who is one of a small handful of managers at the plant. A short half-hour meeting like this takes place each time a team comes back after a few days off. The three men talk about the current pH problem, clear up some items on their list, and spend a little time discussing other interteam concerns such as the status of the maintenance team.

After the meeting, Ed tells his five other team members what he heard in the meeting. He tells Bobby about the pH problem and the UF cleaning that is due. In addition, Maintenance would like some time on the front end.

As he settles into his place in the plant lab, Ed comments on how the people in the PC room control the day. "The people downstairs are there to help, but the guys upstairs make or break the day. If they make good decisions, it'll be a good day. If they make bad decisions, everyone will suffer."

Like all the others, Ed is taking his turn in the rotation: three days in the lab, cooking and analyzing samples of cheese. Everybody on the team has a turn at being the lab technician in every rotation. Everyone learns how to operate this room filled with meters, scales, ovens, centrifuges, desiccators, homogenizers, and blenders, just as everyone learns to push barrels around. In a few days, Ed will move downstairs again, back to those barrels.

Ed's role as communicator shifts to the next team member every month. Until about a year ago, team leadership was supported by personnel outside the team called "team advisers." Now the team assumes those responsibilities, mostly through the communicators, who are the closest thing to team leaders at RGB today.

The plant's basic production process involves removing water from milk, leaving the curd to thicken until it becomes cheese. The milk comes into the plant 12 percent solid and leaves 66 percent solid, looking like still-warm vanilla pudding. The concentration and evaporation operations are always liable to clog the long pipe and vessel system, so frequent cleaning is required. Team members make all the decisions about when and where to clean. Although all the cheese making takes place internally, cleanings call for buckets, hoses, brushes, mops, and elbows.

The graphic representations on his computer screen tell Tim that there is a problem on the back end. He is having trouble discharging from the evaporators. He phones below to Tony, who stops making barrel boxes for a while. Tony calls back minutes later to report that he has found the problem: a clogged check valve. Tony cleans it out and gets it back on line.

Bobby decides to start the UF cleaning early when he finds a broken relief valve. He checks the status of the internal baseline pressure on his computer screen in the PC room, presses a few keys on the keyboard, pockets a wrench with a six-inch span, and heads for the pipes below. Bobby and the automated system perform another cleaning together—caustic ultra-clean, acid wash, and water flush, stage by stage, which takes a few hours. Ted, their newest team member, offers his help. So does Steve from the support team and Sonny, the team's dedicated maintenance person, who suggests that they take extra time now for the thorough UF cleaning that Maintenance sought. They agree, and another level of cleaning begins.

Tim is still having trouble with the evaporator. He tells Bobby, whose UF cleaning job has been largely taken over by the others. Tim's last logged pH reading is so low that it is out of spec. On top of that, downstairs at the spout, Larry has reported some burn-on (caramelized cheese) in the product, so Tim decides to shut down the evaporator right away. Bobby runs downstairs again and this time replaces the filter that Tim pointed to on the screen. All this happens without a word being spoken.

While Bobby is away opening the system, Tim explains the problem to a plant visitor, in plain physical terms, as a gritty substance clogging the filter. He then describes the effect of burn-on to the taste of the product and how they should deal with the barrels that are out of spec. He also talks about the business consequences. It's as if he owns the company—he's an entrepreneur, chef, scientist, troubleshooter, and teacher all in one. He talks about how this problem is likely to affect overall performance for the day, week, and quarter. The evaporator shutdown results in a loss of nine to ten dollars a minute. "Being out of spec," he adds, as he records the occurrence on his log, "also means less incentive payout."

Bobby makes the trip between the gritty filter and Tim's screen three times before the flow is acceptable again. Meanwhile, Tim keeps an eye on Bobby's screen for the status of the UF cleaning operation.

Above those screens, high on one wall in the PC room, is a three-foot-long, Times-Square-like sign that rolls bright red electronic statistics all day: "Congratulations on a very successful third quarter . . . Incentive update . . . Production . . . Conformance goals . . . Turnaround goals . . . Carry-over goals . . . Customer complaints . . ." A bulletin board in the room reports the last period's cumulative turnaround times, nonconformance figures, some pH incentive results, sanitation incentives (various measures for keeping within parameters), plant milk consumption, and evaporator carry-over loss, among other things. Like a refrigerator covered with notes, a nearby marker board holds other reminders: "UF operators: Be sure to get an accurate reading on run sheet: Use 8 quarts of UC II on 1st group . . ." The biggest note in the room is bannered across several feet of continuous computer paper: "Do it right the first time."

Larry is still pushing barrels around under the final output spouts as he talks about teams: "When I first started here, I wasn't sold on the team idea. What I could relate to was the skill-based pay. It stressed that the sharper you are, the faster you can learn, the better you can do, and the sooner you'll be making a lot of money. So I took that to heart.

"What I like best now is the input I can give to management. When I have an idea, it's a direct shot. I feel that no one knows my job better than I do and no one can do it as well as I can. So when I'm asked what the best thing is to do, it's a stroke to my ego.

"There's only one problem with our pay system," Larry continues. "About a year ago, I topped out [learned all the skills in the system and received appropriate compensation increases]." As he stops to label another barrel, he comments that here he is, the highest-paid operator in the plant, and he's down here pushing barrels around half the time. Now that he has topped out, the weight of what to do next shifts to Larry. He says that he still enjoys his work, but he also enjoys tuition reimbursement for a degree in industrial management at Arizona State University.

Employees here are used to talking openly. They continually communicate about their work every day on the job, as well as in an array of team meeting opportunities. Once a month, the Green team holds a special team meeting for about an hour to an hour-and-a-half to talk about what is going on and what will be happening. Team members cover topics such as team goals, vacation schedules, personal needs, interpersonal problems, disciplinary issues, necessary training, committees to be formed, and all the other miscellaneous items that are important to teams and to the company. Special meetings, such as corrective action team meetings, are posted on a large monthly calendar in the hall.

Every Wednesday communicators from each team meet for about an hour for a production meeting that covers operations across the plant. And, like this morning, communicators from relieving teams confer every Monday and Friday. Once a month for an hour-and-a-half to two hours, everybody on the Green team attends an incentive meeting, a get-together where members of the management team share the results of the team and the plant in general and announce the incentive payouts.

With all these meetings, some days stretch out to sixteen hours. One member says it's the price you pay when the only alternative is to let management make all the decisions: "Sometimes you need to make sacrifices. You can't have participation without participation."

About six months ago the Green team took on a new member, a Schreiber veteran. "He started as a parts runner for the company when they were building this place," says Bobby. The man was well respected for his technical ability—so respected, in fact, that the Green team took him on despite his poor attendance record and probationary status. They thought he would work out.

Last month the team made a decision to replace their fellow member. "It's no fun letting someone go," Bobby continues. "He was our friend. We went out with him after work to play ball. We worked with him. We did things for him, and he did things for us. But he fell into a rut where he wasn't meeting his responsibilities. His absences weren't matching his call-ins. He pushed things to the limit. He was clearly over the line, and that was something we had to address. We gave him every opportunity, and basically he didn't respond. So we did what we had to do. It wasn't easy. That was the first time we had to let someone go."

Tony, who has been in teams since Schreiber opened the plant more than five years ago, feels the same way about his former co-worker and friend. "We took a gamble. He had some great ideas, but basically he was lazy. In spite of his good ideas, we were still forced to get rid of him. He's out, and it wasn't easy."

When asked about how careful a team has to be in selecting members, Bobby says that only about 20 percent of the general population would qualify to work in the Green team situation. "Eighty percent wouldn't have the attitude we need. We listen to how a candidate answers our questions for the situations we pose. We look for honesty. If someone is too vague or too uncomfortable when being interviewed by the team, that tells us something too. But we try to make people feel comfortable, and we're systematic in our hiring. We've all been trained on how to interview."

Judy Robinson, the plant's personnel manager, who prefers to call herself "a consultant to the employees," comments on the RGB plant's hiring practices. "I'll have people in the human resource field say to me, 'You mean your *employees* do the interviews?!' I say back to them, 'You mean your *managers and supervisors* do!?!'" Judy told us that team members recently took part in the interviewing process for their new plant manager.

Ted, thirty-six, is the newest Green team member and proud of it. "Where I came from, you couldn't trust people to be here all night by themselves and do the job. When I got here, I knew that this was just up my alley. I don't need a boss looking over my shoulder because I know how to do the work. It never made sense to me to see grown-ups standing around watching other grown-ups do their jobs. I could see it if you were fourteen years old. But I'm an adult, and Schreiber respects that."

Bobby calls it a "cake day." He tells the young woman from the Silver team, his relief, what happened on the front end during the day and informs her when she can expect to start up again. He talks about the silo that is almost ready to come back on line and the one that is ready to go.

Tim tells his replacement how much time is left on the evaporator's CIP, how they treated the system for the pH problem, and that the Silver team should be ready to run at capacity by midnight.

The people downstairs, who packed eighty-two barrels today, are reporting two complete CIP turnarounds and one sanitized barrel room fill area. Meanwhile, Ed fills in Silver's lab person on the latest developments just prior to walking out of the lab.

The Green team is going home.

## THE GREEN TEAM IS A MODEL— OF SORTS

In many ways Schreiber Foods' RGB teams are representative of thousands of self-directed work teams in operation today. The Green team typifies how teams magnify employee empowerment. It is dedicated to quality, and everyone is a master at Schreiber's entire production process. In large part, the leadership role is handled by the team. There are a few things to remember, however, when considering how a Schreiber-like team would work at your location:

- Schreiber was a "greenfield" (start-up) facility. Because some habits are hard to break, start-ups present some advantages in the move toward self-direction that are not present in existing facilities attempting the same transition.

- Schreiber's progressive culture, which places a high value on empowerment, was conducive to a self-directed work teams design. Not all organizations embrace a team approach as Schreiber did.

- Schreiber's RGB plant manager had a lot to do with making teams work at his location. He had a vision from the beginning and refused to be satisfied with the status quo of the manufacturing environment. He believed in high involvement, and he personally facilitated the creation of a work team culture. Having someone on hand to champion empowerment is a real plus—even a must—for successful implementation.

- This plant, with fifty-three associates, is relatively small. While no research data exist, many practitioners contend that smaller facilities are more conducive to high-involvement, team-oriented cultures—perhaps one of the reasons why many manufacturing facilities are working toward smaller manufacturing units. For example, Bill Gore, inventor of Gore-Tex®, keeps all his facilities staffed with fewer than 250 people. Similarly, other larger operations are giving way to factories within factories, or "manufacturing cells." Strength in numbers doesn't necessarily apply to self-directed teams.

- RGB's team culture evolved over time. While there was—and still is—a strong, clear vision of worker empowerment, there was no identifiable point at which self-direction occurred. Leadership responsibility moved downward over several years. And associates are still learning, every day, how to manage themselves better.

PART

II

PREPARING
FOR
TEAMS

I n this part of the book, we move from the empowered team concept to design and implementation. Our primary theme: Teams are a major shift in the way we think of work. As such, carefully planned implementations, executed in concert with overall business objectives, are a must.

We start this part by exploring the role senior management plays in creating a vision for change. Teams must be tied to strategic business objectives and fit within the context of an organization's current value system. With this in mind, the team readiness survey at the end of Chapter Five can help you assess how well teams might work in your company. Next, in Chapter Six, we review the spe-

cific steps involved in designing and implementing teams. Specifically, we discuss the process of work design, the formation and roles of the steering committee and design team, and implementation planning. We also discuss the differences between team implementations in start-up ("greenfield") and existing organizations.

One of the most critical issues facing an organization moving to teams, as we discuss in Chapter Seven, is the role of the "formal" leader. The team concept means a massive role change not only for team members, but for supervisors and managers who must give up the trappings of formal power and learn to lead through empowerment. Some find that it isn't an easy transition to make.

Finally, we get into the specific "how-to's" of selecting and training team members and leaders. Many organizations that have moved to teams direct considerable energy and resources to ensuring the selection of the "right people" for team success. In Chapter Eight, we share the types of selection systems these organizations have designed and how you can go about implementing such a system in your organization.

Working hand in hand with selection, most organizations have established extensive training plans to augment their move to teams. In Chapter Nine, we discuss the types of training needed for both team members and leaders and show you a model of a comprehensive team training plan.

Each chapter in this part includes tips and recommendations you can apply to your own team implementations as you get up and running.

# IMPLEMENTING A NEW VISION:

## The Role of Senior Management

Are self-directed work teams right for your organization? If so, how can you best get them off the ground? Answers to these questions must be thought out well in advance of implementation. Indeed, teams might not be right for all organizations; some that have tried teams warn that to be successful, the team concept must fit into the larger organizational culture and be compatible with the organization's overall business objectives. A recent article in *Industry Week* (Verespej, 1990) warned: "All too often corporate chieftains read the success stories and ordain their companies to adopt work teams—NOW. Work teams don't always work and may even be the wrong solution to the situation in question" (p. 104).

Strategic decisions involving the move to teams usually are made by three groups: senior management, a steering committee, and a design team. The role of *senior management* is to articulate the vision for the organization; decide whether teams should be the subject of further study; and provide the steering committee and design team with overall guidance for future investigation, design, and implementation of teams. The *steering committee* takes the overall vision and direction provided by senior management and oversees the design effort. The *design team* plans the implementation strategy and acts as the ongoing champion of the team process both during the difficult initial birth of teams and during their growth through adolescence to maturity. The specific responsibilities of the steering committee and the design team are covered more fully in Chapter Six.

## MAKING THE INVESTMENT DECISION

Your organization must deal with some broad issues before a steering committee is ever formed. Specifically, senior management needs to accomplish three things:

1. Assess the organization's long-term business needs, defining the role and importance of teams within the larger business context.

2. Determine if the organization's vision (mission) and values are sufficiently clear and compatible to enable empowered teams to operate. (If not, appropriate actions must be taken.)

3. Define the membership and responsibilities of the steering committee.

The following sections will deal with each of these key issues in greater depth.

## WHAT ARE YOUR ORGANIZATION'S LONG-TERM BUSINESS NEEDS?

Some organizations start teams because they're a hot new trend, because teams are working at the company next door, or because the competition is trying it. However, these reasons are insufficient. Teams are not ends in themselves; they are a means by which to achieve other organizational goals.

Organizations consider self-directed teams for a variety of reasons. Some people assume that organizations adopt teams as a last-resort survival mechanism, while in fact, most organizations that undertake the change are already quite healthy. For instance, when Aid Association for Lutherans first considered reorganizing into teams, it did so to accommodate rapid growth in a particular market.

Whatever the original impetus might be, it is important to consider the external business environment the organization will face over the next five to ten years. Senior management has to examine factors such as competitive pressures, changing customer demands, regulatory influences, and potential new product developments. These factors become part of what is called an *environment scan* (a concept explored in the next chapter). This scan analyzes *who* in the outside world expects *what* of the organization, and it helps to shape decisions about the need and reasons for self-directed teams.

Senior management also must agree on the results or goals expected in each of these areas:

- *Direct business reasons for teams.* What bottom-line business indexes (scrap rate, quality, customer service ratings, reduced cycle time, etc.) will be affected by adopting teams? What will improvement in the indexes mean to the overall success and competitiveness of the organization?

- *Indirect business reasons for teams.* What changes can be expected in indirect business indexes (improvement in morale, less employee turnover, fewer union grievances)? These indirect reasons obviously interact with the direct reasons.

- *Investment required to implement and maintain teams.* Is the cost worth it? Comparing the relationship of anticipated benefits with costs determines the change effort's return on investment.

## THINKING THROUGH THE ISSUES

It is particularly difficult to establish and agree on goals and expectations, because there is a tendency to inflate expectations and underestimate required resources. It is easy to be swayed by statistics reported in the business literature that describe situations where teams increased productivity or quality substantially, decreased costs, or tripled customer service indexes. There are many reasons, however, why these publicized results may be poor goal-setting guides.

For example, negative results are seldom published; only the most positive are quoted by business magazines. And, as mentioned in the prologue, few effectiveness reports actually represent controlled scientific studies. Organizations almost always make a number of changes as teams are being put in place. They may provide more training, for instance, or add quality improvement processes, or install new equipment at the same time as the team implementation. Therefore, the results that are achieved may well be affected by other changes that are—or are not—being made along with the move to teams.

It is our experience that measurable improvements take a considerable amount of time and may yield more modest results than some reports would have you believe.

When estimating the possible impact of empowered teams on operations, an organization must consider its current situation. This includes the degree of empowerment felt by individuals *without* teams and the present level of productivity, quality, and customer service. The organization's history of accepting changes, the morale of those who will be involved, and the impact of other organizational events such as new products, relocations, and layoffs also need to be considered.

Estimating resource requirements can be difficult. There will be out-of-pocket expenses for travel, facility redesign, and training programs, as well as indirect costs for such items as site visits, meetings, training, and facilitators.

You also must consider lost opportunity costs from similar investments in other areas of productivity, quality, or customer service enhancements. An added difficulty is that some teams experience an initial decrease in productivity or quality before improvements occur. Generally, this is related to the degree of disruption caused by new layouts, equipment, responsibilities, and procedures. These costs (referred to as "ramp-up" costs) often are factored into a start-up but may be neglected in an established organization that is converting to teams.

In considering these issues, it is important to remember that none of the decisions made by senior management can be precise. Yet it is important for clear, bottom-line expectations to start at the top of the organization. At that point, the steering committee can refine benefit and cost estimates.

Determining an anticipated return on investment from teams is fundamental to deciding whether teams will be advantageous. Unfortunately, too many organizations fail to think these issues through before taking the plunge.

## ARE YOUR VISION AND VALUES SUFFICIENTLY CLEAR AND UNDERSTOOD?

One of the biggest challenges leaders face today is translating their vision—or mission—into reality and persuading people at all levels of the organization to pull together to achieve common goals. Visioning in an empowered organization is a special challenge that is an essential first step to a successful transition to teams. As Figure 5.1 indicates, a clear vision establishes the foundation for effective, efficient change that eventually results in the team making clear, informed decisions.

In an empowered organization, the best guidance comes from the team's understanding of the organization's vision and values. It cannot come from rules or books of procedures; that is *not* empowerment. No book of procedures can answer all the questions that arise, and manuals are quickly outdated. The *vision* of the organization tells the team in which direction the organization is going and what it plans to accomplish. The organization's *values* tell the team how to accomplish the vision. Values are the subtle control mechanisms that informally sanction or prohibit behavior.

An organization's culture develops from its most salient values. To achieve responsible, informed decision making at the

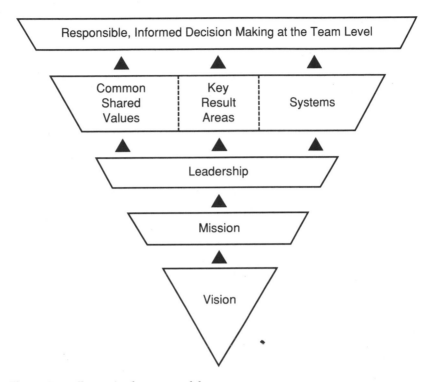

**Figure 5.1.** Strategic change model.

lowest possible levels of the organization, everyone must understand the organization's vision and values. As Robert Hass, CEO of Levi Strauss and Company, put it: "In a more volatile and dynamic business environment, the controls have to be conceptual. It's the ideas of a business that are controlling, not some manager with authority. Values provide a common language for aligning a company's leadership and its people" (Howard, 1990, p. 134).

Ancient traders used a "touchstone" to determine the purity of gold and silver. They would rub metal on their touchstone and determine that metal's purity by examining the streak left on the stone. In other words, the touchstone served as a guide to decision making. Similarly, values can be considered touchstones for judgment within an organization. A team that is faced with a quality or customer service decision has to turn to its basic understanding of the way management wants the organization to operate. Team members should "touch" the values of the organization.

For example, in one automobile company, *quality* is the overriding value. Any team member can shut down the assembly line if quality is thought to be compromised. At one car per minute, that is an expensive decision for an employee to make. But if you walked around the plant for just ten minutes, you would know that quality is the company's key value. Statistical process control charts cover the workplace. Cars with quality problems are left in the middle of the floor so that teams can take their time to explore the factors that caused the problems in the first place. Problem-solving meetings are taking place all the time.

In the early stages of considering whether to implement teams, it is extremely important for the organization to confront the status of its vision and values. At this time two questions must be answered:

1. Are the vision and values conducive to having empowered teams?

2. Are the vision and values clearly understood by people in the organization?

If the organization's vision and values are not appropriate and widely internalized, it is unrealistic to expect teams to operate at high levels of empowerment.

## DEVELOPING A VISION AND VALUES

If you are missing a clear vision and a set of values, you may have some work ahead of you before starting teams. There are many methods of developing a vision (mission) statement and defining values. Most frequently, an off-site workshop is effective. The purpose of this meeting is to define a vision statement (if the organization doesn't already have one), a single driving value for the organization, and supporting or facilitating values.

It is important to define the driving value because cultural values often conflict with each other. For example, the values of product quality and customer service might conflict when the organization tries to meet a customer's need for fast delivery. Getting the product out the door quickly might mean compromising quality. Similarly, product quality might conflict with profit when research and development projects exceed their budgets. In this case, one value may be compromised. Unfortunately, many organizations mistakenly ignore conflicts among values and try to instill too many values simultaneously (we recently came across a pharmaceutical company with fourteen key values). We think that four to six are a "manageable" number of values. Through a series of highly interactive sessions, the senior management team can identify the organization's driving value and define several supporting or facilitating values.

Figure 5.2 shows the vision and values from I/N Tek, a new plant representing a venture between Inland Steel Industries and Nippon Steel. The statement took many months (and people) to compose and refine.

Defining the vision and values, which is a challenge in itself, is only the first step in creating an empowered culture. Next, the vision and values must be communicated throughout the organization in a way that builds commitment and meaning. We have been in dozens of companies with vision or mission statements and values posted all around. Yet most employees, when they were asked, could not repeat their organization's mission or list its values.

In addition, the organization must give serious consideration to its systems and processes to be sure they reflect and reinforce its values. System congruence will occur as a natural outcome of the team design process explained in the next chapter, providing

---

### I/N Tek Mission

The I/N Tek mission is to produce the most marketable cold-reduced products sold in the United States, maintaining the highest standards in quality, cost, and consumer satisfaction through the integration of human resources, equipment, technology, and business systems while providing secure and satisfying employment and an attractive return to investors.

### I/N Tek Values

**Quality Focus**

We will commit our individual abilities and team efforts to achieve the highest-quality results in all aspects of personal performance, the productive process, and all functions of the organization.

**Customer Orientation**

We will seek out and satisfy our customers' needs and constantly strive to exceed their expectations. We recognize that the quality of our products has a powerful impact on our customers' manufacturing process and the quality of their products.

**Constant Improvement** *(Kaizen)*

We will continually strive to find better ways to do our work and to grow as individuals.

**Participation and Involvement**

We will seek input to find the best solutions to problems and methods of making improvements in the workplace. We will share information, resources, and ideas, and we will develop the skills necessary to maintain an exciting work environment where decisions are made at the lowest appropriate level.

**People Focus**

We will ensure a cooperative partnership among all members of I/N Tek in a framework built on mutual trust, respect, and a sense of dignity. We will provide opportunities for all employees to reach their maximum potential and to experience more secure and satisfying employment in a safe and healthy environment.

**Cost Consciousness**

We will continually improve operating efficiency and reduce costs based on the recognition that every action we take can influence external as well as internal costs.

---

**Figure 5.2.** Sample mission statement for I/N Tek. Reprinted courtesy of I/N Tek.

the design team uses the organization's vision and values as its foundation.

## WHO IS ON THE STEERING COMMITTEE AND WHAT ARE ITS RESPONSIBILITIES?

After the decision to establish teams is reaffirmed, it is time to consider the makeup and responsibilities of the steering committee, which will oversee the design effort. There are a few natural candidates for this committee: the senior managers of the unit where teams will be located; local (or national) union leaders; functional managers (such as those in Engineering or Human Resources); and, in many cases, first-line leaders and line associates who might be affected by the change.

In preparation for a team implementation, it is often desirable for steering committee members to visit other organizations that are using teams, to read articles about teams, and, in various other ways, to gain insight into the team concept. Be careful, though: A common mistake stemming from visiting organizations that are successfully using self-directed work teams is the tendency to be so impressed by the design of a particular site that an organization adopts the same structure without considering all available options. Like any other important decision, it is useful to consider an array of possibilities before deciding on specific methods for your particular organization.

## MANAGING RESISTANCE AND CHANGE

No change comes without resistance, and this is certainly the case with self-directed teams; nor does every work team story have a happy ending. Parker and Slaughter (1988) recently presented a rather one-sided union "anti-team" view. In their book, they review some team applications that have ended in failure. Those failures, in our opinion, occurred not so much because of any inherent "evil" in teams (as the authors seem to propose) but because management did not anticipate the magnitude of the change it was asking its organization to make. Similarly, Wysocki (1990) reviewed a less-than-successful "bottom-up" team approach at a Pratt & Whitney plant in Maine. (Other Pratt & Whitney plants have since instituted very successful team implementations.) Again, the change process was a major culprit in the failed implementation.

Teams represent a major shift in the way an organization produces its products and values its people. As is the case with any major culture change, the buy-in and support of those who will be affected by the change should be considered carefully, early, and up front. Often the job of managing this change, at least initially, falls on the shoulders of senior management.

Earlier in this chapter we talked about the role of senior managers in creating and communicating a vision and values for their new team-based organizations. This is an important part of the change process—but only a part. It is often important to conduct some sort of organization-wide "kickoff" before a team implementation process begins. The purpose of this type of event is to give everyone a better feel for the team concept, present a quick overview of the key actions and timing, and offer an explanation regarding why the organization is moving toward teams.

These sessions often tend to focus on organizational benefits rather than on WIIFMs (What's In It For Me?), which obviously are far more important. These WIIFMs might include greater earning potential, task variety, job control, and participation in organizational decisions. This is a good time to tackle the issue of job security as well. If you can't provide reassurances about relatively stable employment, you at least need to make it clear that if layoffs occur, it will not be because of the team implementation. As we will discuss in Chapter Seven, it is a good idea to hold these sessions initially with middle managers and/or first-line leaders before the work force is included as a whole. Enlisting their assistance and support first will help the change process go more smoothly.

In addition to WIIFMs, it is a good idea to have mechanisms in place that allow people to share their anxieties and receive straight answers to questions. This type of support can range from open question-and-answer sessions to special support sessions for supervisors (a strategy successfully implemented at the Adolph Coors Company's warehouse operations). It is also important to let associates know that they are not expected to make the change without support. For example, everyone should understand that with new skill requirements will come appropriate training and on-the-job coaching.

Finally, in creating the vision, senior management should delegate to others in the organization as many of the ''how-to's'' as possible. Involvement in the actual change process by the union, managers, and employees will manifest itself as a heightened sense of ownership in the team concept and will increase the odds for successful implementation.

## TEAM TIPS

Following are some lessons we have discovered that can help you as you go about establishing a vision for teams in your organization.

## Make Sure Your Vision Is Real

Visions must be tied to solid business activities; they must be customer driven, people focused, and value based. Unless your hopes

and aspirations are related realistically to business goals and operations, they will be difficult for people to grasp, and they may never
find their way into everyday practice.

## Make the Effort to Communicate the Vision

Make sure that in formulating your vision, you spend time planning how you will communicate and model it. Always be prepared
to talk personally about the vision, refer to it when making major
business decisions, and, above all, model the values you establish.

## Pay Attention to Your Current Culture

Teams receive such good press today that many managers read
an article or two and decide to start teams of their own. Teams
work, however, only when an organization's culture is ready for
them. This readiness can be determined by looking at how the
organization treats its people. Are employees trusted and asked
for their opinions? Are individuals allowed to try new things? Is
there a fundamental respect for everyone's contributions? Is there
a good relationship between management and labor?

# ARE YOU READY FOR
# SELF-DIRECTED WORK TEAMS?

In order to determine your organization's cultural receptivity to
teams, you should conduct some sort of *readiness assessment*. An
example of such an assessment is given in Figure 5.3. A readiness
assessment does not have to be an exhaustive, comprehensive

## Team Readiness Survey

**Question:** When does it make sense to start work teams in your organization?

**Answer:** When the conditions are right.

To help you determine how conducive your organization is to the implementation of teams, you might want to give some thought to key situational issues. Using the scale below each item, give yourself a "5" for *yes* (if you strongly agree with the item), a "1" for *no* (if you strongly disagree with the item), or a "2," "3," or "4" depending on how close you are to either end of the scale. When you are finished, total your scores for an indication of your organization's readiness to accept work teams.

1. Management believes that front-line employees can and should make the majority of decisions that affect how they do their work.

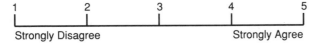

2. Employees can suggest and implement improvements to their work without going through several levels of approval.

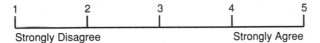

3. The union is likely to agree to renegotiate traditional work rules and job classifications to permit greater flexibility and autonomy.

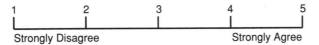

4. The nature of the work in your organization lends itself to a team-based approach rather than to individual effort.

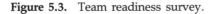

**Figure 5.3.** Team readiness survey.

5. Your technology is flexible enough to permit restructuring or reorganization based on the needs of your teams. The physical design of your workplace lends itself to working in teams.

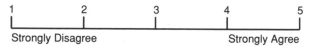

6. It is possible to organize work so that teams of employees can take responsibility for entire jobs.

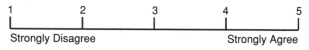

7. There is enough complexity in jobs to allow for initiative and decision making.

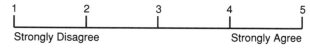

8. Your employees would be interested or willing to organize into teams.

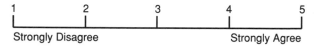

9. Your overall organizational culture, vision, and values support teamwork and empowerment.

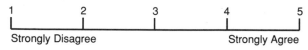

10. Your organization has a history of following through on initiatives such as empowerment.

**Figure 5.3—***Continued*

11. Management in your organization is willing to adjust responsibility downward and radically change its own roles and behavior.

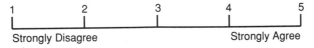

12. Your company is secure enough to guarantee a period of relative stability during which the teams can develop.

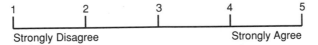

13. You have adequate support functions, such as human resources, engineering, and maintenance, that can help teams by providing information, coaching, and training.

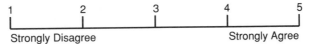

14. Management understands that developing teams is a lengthy, time-consuming, and labor-intensive process. It is willing and able to make the investment.

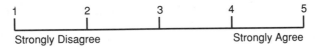

15. Your organization has systems that provide timely information to front-line employees.

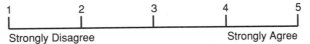

**Figure 5.3**—*Continued*

16. Your employees have the skills needed to take greater control of their jobs.

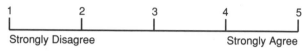

17. You are willing to invest in training your front-line employees.

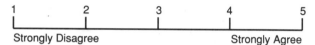

Your Total Score: _____

| Score* | Actions* |
|---|---|
| Above 65 | You are on solid ground. Teams stand a good chance of taking root if properly implemented. |
| Between 40 and 64 | There are some weaknesses in your culture's policies, processes, and procedures. Try to work on the weak areas before going ahead with a team implementation. |
| Below 40 | Teams will have difficulty taking hold. You need to reexamine your culture and possibly explore a more gradual course toward empowerment before implementing self-directed teams. |

*Scores/Actions are guidelines only. Questions do not carry equal weight in every organization.

**Figure 5.3**—*Continued*

analysis. However, you do need to ask (and answer) a number of key questions about your organization's culture, practices, and goals. If you can answer these questions in the affirmative, you are ready for teams and should begin putting empowered teams in place. To get an initial feel for your organization's readiness to incorporate work teams, try the exercise shown in Figure 5.3.

CHAPTER

6

# PLANNING THE SUCCESSFUL LAUNCH OF SELF-DIRECTED TEAMS:
## The Design Process and Principles

Once you decide to establish self-directed teams in your organization, you face the challenge of turning vision into reality. This chapter covers some of the basics of getting up and running: the team design process, implementation, ongoing assessment, and evaluation.

For teams to work most effectively, a company will need to change the way work is designed just as it must modify various organizational

| Vision | Design | Implementation | Monitoring |
|---|---|---|---|
| Envision the future. | Assess the current versus the desired state: | Assess readiness; plan roll-out. | Evaluate: <br> • Attitudes <br> • Performance |
| Create awareness of the need for change: <br> • Read the literature. <br> • Visit other sites. <br> • Scan the environment. | • Technical analysis <br> • Social analysis | Provide orientation and training. | Renew: <br> • Awareness <br> • Commitment <br> • Skills |
| | Optimize technical and social systems in tentative design. | Reevaluate design and make needed changes. | Redesign, if appropriate. |
| Clarify the mission, vision, and values for the organization. | Examine and, if appropriate, change the organizational system. | | |
| Make a commitment by setting goals and objectives. | Agree on process and result measures. | | |
| Involve key stakeholders: <br> • Steering committee <br> • Design team | Develop a plan for moving forward. | | |

**Figure 6.1.** Team design process.

systems to support that design. It is also necessary to develop and execute a change plan.

Almost everyone in your organization will be important to the success of a team implementation. Keep in mind that any implementation can stray a bit off course. For this reason, you must evaluate progress continually, making changes along the way in order to keep on track. Figure 6.1 illustrates each of the key stages of initiating teams.

# DESIGN PRINCIPLES

Ownership of work (empowerment), which is the heart of self-directed teams, often requires taking a new look at the way work is performed, and at the systems that support the work. More than fifteen years ago, Cherns (1976) presented fundamentals of work design that still apply today.'

## Minimal Critical Specification (Keep It Simple)

The wisdom here is: Don't specify any more than is absolutely necessary. Don't create any more rules, regulations, or general bureaucracy than you need. Traditionally, organizations are encrusted with rules and regulations that act like barnacles slowing the progress of a ship. Overly complex procedures can be unhealthy, especially when your goal is to have teams assume responsibility for their business, adapt to customer needs, and increase flexibility.

## Multifunctionalism (Task Variety)

Rather than performing only a highly specialized job, each individual team member should be able to understand and perform all the tasks within the team. Multifunctionalism (or multiskilling) helps teams adapt to changing demands. For example, assemblers at Litton Industries' Utah facility perform inspections, test functions, and handle master production control.

## Boundary Location (Job Ownership)

Whenever possible, give your teams a whole and identifiable piece of the business with complete responsibility for producing a product or service. The value of this idea contrasts with traditional forms of job design where *equipment* or *territories* are the guiding principles. For example, many organizations are set up like machine shops with all the grinding machines in one room and all the milling machines in another. A lot of time is wasted shuffling products back and forth between departments. We have also seen assembly lines where people in a certain geographic area are called a "team" even though they have no identifiable joint responsibility. Misusing the term, of course, fails to inspire people to take ownership of the business.

## Information Flow (Open Communication)

Information systems should be designed to provide information directly to the point where action on the data occurs. The Japanese *Kanban* visual inventory systems are a good example. These systems provide teams with instant visual information on the status of parts. At one Midwest manufacturing facility, production costs and sales information are shared with the teams on a daily basis. This is quite a departure from traditional systems that provide such information only to managers.

## Support Congruence (Empowering Systems)

Often existing organizational systems—rewards, training, and time-keeping systems, for example—will undermine your vision and values. In such cases, these systems must be redesigned to reinforce rather than subvert the team process. We have seen procedures still on the books that were designed to prevent an occurrence that happened once, perhaps twenty years ago. These kinds of obsolete systems and high degrees of control can interfere with team behavior, and make little sense today.

## Evolution (Fine Tuning)

Team design never ends. Remember that a team's emergence is *evolutionary*, not *revolutionary*. Don't expect to create a perfect design in six days. Instead, plan to reevaluate and adjust your design constantly. Lake Superior Paper Industries is still redesigning its teams three years into the team implementation.

# DESIGNING TEAMS

Most successful team implementations involve people at all organizational levels; in fact, those closest to the work are often in the best position to recommend design changes. Figure 6.2 illustrates the degree of involvement for major stakeholders in the design process. The more *all* stakeholders are involved in the design and implementation process, the more likely it is that your teams will be successful.

To ensure that the design proceeds in a timely and organized fashion, a *steering committee* and a *design team* are often established to oversee and implement the design.

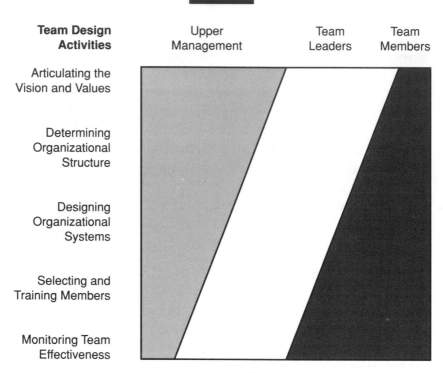

**Figure 6.2.** Stakeholders' involvement in the design process.

# THE STEERING COMMITTEE

As discussed in Chapter Five, the steering committee is the initial planning group and serves as an umbrella for the entire team design process. This committee typically consists of upper and middle management, collective bargaining representatives, facilitators, individuals who will serve the teams as leaders and coaches, and in some cases a sample of prospective team members.

The steering committee tends to meet frequently early in the process; later it meets only when the design team needs its approval or guidance. The role of this committee is to champion the team design process in visible ways, including:

- Clarifying and communicating the organization's vision and values (with senior management)

- Developing a charter that spells out the purpose and importance of teams

- Providing a link to the larger organization's needs and policies

- Protecting the design process from any dysfunctional influences

- Providing general support (including resources) for implementation

In one automotive products company we worked with, the steering committee played a particularly valuable role as a bridge to the rest of the organization. Division management had a seemingly persistent desire to test and meddle in one plant's team design. It went beyond the usual question—"What are you guys up to, anyway?"—and began to approach sabotage of the plant's plans. When the divisional accounting director told the plant that it was not allowed to simplify traditional accounting reports for the teams' use, the steering committee stepped in. The committee organized awareness training at division headquarters, and key division managers were invited to tour the plant. Eventually, team members were making monthly presentations at divisional meetings. The steering committee had opened the lines of communication and prevented further conflict.

## THE DESIGN TEAM

How involved the steering committee becomes in the design process varies. Since it can be a time-consuming effort, many steering committees delegate the actual implementation to a design team. The design team might include members of the steering committee, but it also has a broader representation of supervisors, team members, union officials, human resource practitioners, and, if required, functional experts from areas such as Engineering or Management Information Systems. Usually the design team is responsible for designing, implementing, monitoring, and hammering out the details of self-directed teams. Questions they address include:

- How will teams be structured?

- What will the team boundaries be?

- What tasks will the teams be responsible for?

- What outcomes or results of the teams' efforts will be measured?

- How can the facilities be arranged to support team functioning?

- How will the teams get the information they need to manage their business?

- Where will the teams meet?

- What training will the teams need?

- How will the reward systems support the organization's values?

- How will the design team keep the teams on track and "renew" the process?

- How will the teams assess their performance?

# THE DESIGN PROCESS

Many design teams go through a process known as *sociotechnical analysis,* a process with many variations. As the name implies, a sociotechnical analysis is a combination of social and technical variables. Regardless of the type of analysis, the goal is the same: designing the organization in a way that optimizes social, technical, and administrative systems to achieve business objectives.

This section describes four of the key steps involved in an organizational design effort:

1. Technical analysis
2. Social analysis
3. Joint optimization
4. Agreement on process and result measures

## Technical Analysis

Some design teams start with an *environment scan,* although parts of a scan may have been completed previously by senior management or the steering committee. (As explained earlier, an environment scan is an analysis of who deals with an organization and what they expect of that organization.) In the customer service department of one electronics manufacturer, for instance, the design team surveyed the expectations of employees in the company production facilities and the field sales offices, as well as current external customers. They also analyzed the competition's market share, projected economic fluctuations, and forecasted business growth. Based on this information, the design team ensured that the newly formed teams would be able to meet customer requirements and accommodate a 20 percent expected annual growth in the operation.

Next, the design team analyzed the process and technology that would be used, by identifying the *major unit operations.* (We picked a simple example: filling a book order. It is common to see many more unit operations than we talk about here in a complex service or manufacturing process.) Major unit operations consist of a series of activities that results in a tangible output, as shown in Table 6.1.

In our example, once the process was clear, the design team analyzed each activity in every operation for value-added activities. If the activity did not contribute significantly to meeting customer requirements, it was redesigned or eliminated. In this case, the team eliminated thirteen different tasks, including one lengthy report that had been required by the former inventory manager. Her replacement had been receiving the report and discarding it for over nine months.

Next, the design team identified key variances (potential work flow disturbances) that could critically affect the desired output. In our example, the customer service department had misunderstood the urgency of a customer's need. This is a variance that often occurs in the first unit operation, when the request is ini-

**TABLE 6.1**
**An Example of Major Unit Operations**

| Major Unit Operation | Tangible Output |
|---|---|
| 1. Receive request for product ...... ➤ | Complete initial request form |
| 2. Accept request ................ ➤ | Document information needed to fill an order |
| 3. Book order .................... ➤ | Confirm pricing to customer and sales department |
| 4. Ship order .................... ➤ | Confirm at headquarters and with customer |

tially received; the request is not controlled or checked until the fourth unit of operation, requiring extensive adjustment of the shipping schedule.

One purpose of the technical analysis is to structure teams so that the occurrence of key variances is controlled within the team. In this example, rather than maintaining an order-entry group that received and accepted requests, plus a shipping group that booked and shipped products, teams were formed by sales region and enjoyed complete ownership of the process for their customers, from initial request to shipping the order. An additional major benefit of the reorganization was that the service representatives became much more collaborative and in tune with both the territory sales staff and their customer base.

In a particularly innovative application of this design process, the San Diego Zoo recently reorganized one of its new exhibits (Blines, 1990). The zoo was constructing a bioclimatic zone (a grouping of plants and animals from a particular region of the world) and saw the opportunity to create a team design in its new "Tiger River" exhibit. Rather than having different functional departments take care of cleaning, maintenance, plants, reptiles, and so on, team members were cross-trained and given responsibility for the entire exhibit. At Tiger River a horticultural specialist might be seen washing windows, and everyone pitches in to keep the grounds clean. Guest experiences at this exhibit were once rated at 4.4 on a 10-point scale. Now they have risen to 8.3. Quality of work life was rated 6.0, while today it is 9.8.

## Social Analysis

A good analysis of a social system at work requires the mapping out of roles and responsibilities in order to create jobs with meaningful content. A key component of a social analysis is a close look at tasks that are usually reserved for supervisors and managers in order to decide how they will be transferred to the team over time.

Chapter Seven examines the transfer of leadership responsibility and presents some tools and techniques for thinking through transfer issues. The major objective is to avoid prematurely loading additional responsibilities on the team before members are technically proficient, willing, and able to assume them. The transfer plan is revised frequently as teams mature and are able to assume more responsibility.

Relations with support departments such as Maintenance, Engineering, Accounting, Purchasing, and Human Resources also should be included in the social analysis. It is important for each support area to examine its work to evaluate what tasks should be turned over to the teams. For example, the Human Resources area may want to give teams full responsibility for interviewing candidates and may be willing to share the responsibility for monitoring Equal Employment Opportunity compliance, but they might prefer to retain full responsibility for conducting external salary surveys.

Clarifying responsibilities up front can save confusion later on. One large hotel chain recently moved toward the team concept, delegating the various floors of its buildings to teams of housekeepers. In the old system, it was not the housekeeper's responsibility to find maintenance problems in the rooms; this was the job of the supervisor who checked the rooms after they had been cleaned. When teams were formed, the supervisor's job was phased out and everyone wondered how this responsibility would be handled. Would the housekeepers call Maintenance directly, or would they produce a central list and send it to Maintenance, as they did before? Who would handle the communication with Maintenance? The problem was not a difficult one to solve; it just required clarity and communication, which the teams were able to accomplish in a single meeting.

Deciding which tasks are reserved for leaders and which for team members is only the beginning. The design team has to determine how the various leadership tasks that are to be assumed by the team will be handled within the team. Lyman Ketchum (1984), one of the pioneers of work design, refers to this challenge as the "everyone-is-responsible-for-everything-while-no-one-is-responsible-for-anything syndrome."

Most organizations avoid this syndrome by introducing some kind of structure to handle their new responsibilities. One approach is known as the STAR structure. In this instance, STAR stands for Situation or Task, Action, Result. Figure 6.3 gives an example of the STAR concept as it is used at Hannaford Brothers Co. Each point on the star represents a function that a team member manages for the team. For each of these functions, there are specific responsibilities and tasks the team member is expected to perform. In most cases, team members rotate through the points on the star quarterly so that all team members eventually learn all aspects of managing their business.

International Bio-Synthetics, a chemical manufacturer in Kingstree, South Carolina, adopted a similar structure called the "Sunshine" approach. Team members take responsibility for different "rays": quality, good manufacturing practices, safety, sanitation, production, maintenance, and administration. Other organizations have come up with different concepts and approaches. All these approaches focus on making sure that the team is covering all the bases as it assumes increasing responsibility for the entire job.

## Joint Optimization

To come up with the best design, the design team must optimize both the social and technical systems to create the most effective organizational structure. The desired results are that teams identify and control variances at their source, coordinate work at the lowest appropriate level, and obtain support from the larger organization's systems.

**Figure 6.3.** STAR concept. Reprinted courtesy of Hannaford Brothers Co.

No non-value-added tasks should remain, and all jobs should have the following basic ingredients for empowerment:

- A complete and meaningful piece of work
- Decision-making responsibility
- Opportunities to exercise initiative
- Use of various skills
- Feedback on performance

This is possible only when the technical and social systems have been analyzed and redesigned simultaneously. For example, after one design team identified the need for more frequent communication between operators, the team changed the layout of the equipment, enabling face-to-face operator communication. If the technical aspects of the design (in this case, equipment layout) had already been determined before the social systems were considered, the result would have been a less-than-optimal design.

## Agreement on Process and Result Measures

Before actual implementation, the design team should agree on the criteria it will use to evaluate the effectiveness of the design. Team progress should be monitored from the start, and the design team should be prepared to intervene when necessary. Methods of monitoring usually involve observation of teams in practice and the occasional use of questionnaires to gain more insight into member satisfaction. Often, hard, bottom-line results do not come instantly (sometimes there may even be an initial downturn in performance indicators); however, measurement should start immediately, as a way of keeping the team's attention focused on organizational goals.

Some common team design measures are outlined in Figure 6.4. In general, these measures are agreed upon with the steering committee and are monitored throughout the process.

## IMPLEMENTATION

Once the design team completes the design process, attention can turn to implementation and change management. Some issues to consider include the following:

- Over what period of time are we going to roll out the team structure?

- What systems must be modified to support the teams?

- What training needs does each of the stakeholder groups have?

- What obstacles might inhibit change? What can we do about these obstacles?

| Process Measures | Result Measures |
|---|---|
| • Adherence to start-up schedule | • Customer satisfaction |
| • Interim climate checks | • Customer quality ratings |
| • In-process personnel turnover | • Productivity |
| • Design team cohesiveness | • Turnaround time |
| | • Inventory levels |
| | • Scrap/rework rates |

**Figure 6.4.**   Team outcome measures.

- What else needs to be done to gain acceptance to the change?

- How will we measure our progress?

In many cases, design teams elect to have subgroups tackle these issues. These subgroups present their recommendations to the full design team to be integrated into a comprehensive implementation plan. The design team can then generate timelines, goals, checkpoints, and key indicators. It is clear that taking the team concept from theory to practice can be time consuming. This is because an implementation plan should be a detailed map of *everything* it takes to get teams started and moving along the continuum toward achieving the vision. All major barriers should be identified, eliminating those that are possible and working around the others.

In almost all cases, in-place organizational systems will work counter to team implementation. These systems must be identified and modified as well.

Some systems worth examining are listed here:

- *Quality practices.* Creating expectations and cultivating skills so that responsibility for quality is built in at the team level

- *Customer contact.* Getting teams in touch with internal and external customers

- *Vendor relations.* Allowing teams to work in partnership with vendors to control quality and costs

- *Selection and promotion.* Teaching teams to select their own members and leaders

- *Training and development.* Planning on extensive social and technical skills training to be phased in over time

- *Compensation and recognition.* Exploring alternative compensation forms, such as pay for skills and gain sharing, that reward team performance

- *Communication.* Opening lines of communication, remembering that effective communication requires time and appropriate internal systems

- *Organizational "symbols."* Eliminating status symbols (such as company cars and special cafeterias)

- *Physical facilities.* Designing with an eye toward effective teamwork (creating physical layouts that encourage interaction, allow for meeting space, etc.)

- *Budgeting.* Planning to involve teams in the budgeting process; allowing for team capital expense decisions

- *Labor relations.* Involving unions *early*

- *Performance management.* Exploring team-based appraisal processes and team member involvement in performance feedback

- *Strategic and long-range planning.* Allowing teams to make contributions to department and company direction.

## ROLLING OUT THE DESIGN

There are essentially three ways of launching a design in the organization:

1. Creating a pilot area
2. Phased-in conversion
3. Total immersion

Each approach comes with its own set of advantages and disadvantages, but we have seen all three work. Typically, total immersion is used in start-ups or specially organized *focused* cells within larger factories. Pilots and phased-in conversions are more common in up-and-running organizations. Table 6.2 shows these three options.

If you choose to implement teams in a selected area of your operation, try to look for a site with the following characteristics:

- Supportive and naturally empowering managers

- Employees with an interest in greater involvement

- An anticipated change in a product or process

- A reasonably healthy bottom line that can tolerate possible changeover productivity problems

Avoid areas that:

- Offer no possibility for social interaction

- Have been the subject of innumerable management ''programs''

- Are susceptible to comments like "If it works here, it'll work anywhere"

There are other important considerations in pilot implementations, such as appropriate, early-on communication. In one large Canadian paper operation, a new mill was added to a major plant. The employees in the addition began operating as self-directed work teams while the employees in the larger, older portion of the plant continued to operate under traditional methods. All the employees ate in the same cafeteria, and many were friends away

**TABLE 6.2**
**Roll-Out Options**

| Type of Implementation | Advantages | Disadvantages |
|---|---|---|
| Pilot area (single, self-directed team) | • Easy to start<br>• Easy to control | • Feelings of isolation (being in a fishbowl)<br>• Difficult for team to share problems and learn from others<br>• Other areas of the organization feel neglected |
| Phased-in conversion | • Moderately easy to manage<br>• Design team learns as it goes | • Confusing to juggle traditional systems with new systems over time<br>• Requires more planning |
| Total immersion | • No one feels left out<br>• All systems change at once (no need to maintain dual systems) | • Requires the most planning<br>• May be unsettling and confusing<br>• Entails the most risk<br>• Requires the most commitment |

from the worksite. To those outside the team-converted area, it seemed that the team members had easier jobs. They did not have bosses to watch them all the time. To others, it seemed that they had harder jobs because they were more active and attended meetings before and after their shifts. Tensions grew that could have been avoided with better up-front communication.

## MONITORING THE IMPLEMENTATION

Monitoring is an ongoing process that requires continual dedication of both the design team and up-and-running work teams. We have yet to come across an implementation that did not require change along the way. Rapidly changing technologies, market demands, and organizational maturity force constant reevaluation. Unfortunately, two powerful countervailing forces often prevent the design team from adequately monitoring team functioning:

1. It is very tempting to kick back and relax after a long and involved design and implementation phase.

2. It is perhaps even more tempting to rush out and "convert" another area before taking the time to learn and improve.

Because the early stages of team development are critical, it is important to evaluate them closely. This is the time when the most ambiguity and frustration occur, but it is also the time when it might be relatively painless to make changes—before teams are "frozen" into new ways of doing things.

Evaluation can be accomplished in a number of ways. The most common is the use of observation and interviews with team members. Another involves administering questionnaires to determine group cohesiveness and satisfaction with the team concept (see Figure 13.1 for an example). The design team should hold meetings regularly to check the progress of its teams. The development of teams within organizations should be managed like any other activity: through measurement and a continued commitment to improvement.

When monitoring shows early problems, try to avoid acting hastily to change major parts of the implementation plan such as the team design. Some organizations fail to give their initial design enough time to work; they start making corrections right away. Often these adjustments turn out to be worse than the original problem. We have seen many teams diverge from their initial plan only to revert to the same plan a year later.

Measurement of a team's performance and movement toward empowerment should not be used as a basis for individual evaluation early on. Treat it instead as an *aid* in the continuing development of the team. Some of the initial changes you do see—such as climate changes and productivity/quality indicators—are quite amenable to measurement. Collect and communicate these data because they will act as an early reinforcement for the use of teams. And, in the full spirit of empowerment, encourage your teams to measure and report their own progress.

The true test of teams—and management's commitment to teams—usually comes during rush times; changeovers; the introduction of new technology; or the loss of key team members, team leaders, and group leaders. If there is a weak point in the fabric, situations like these will tear it. Quick mending is a must, or the strength of the whole effort is at risk.

## A Few Words About Start-Ups Versus Existing Organizations

The problems of implementing teams differ from place to place depending on the cultural and emotional baggage at each location.

While work teams have prospered in many types of organizations —from a 100-year-old unionized furniture manufacturer with a history of labor unrest to an established, member-owned insurance company—the formula for creating empowered teams differs depending on the degree and type of changes that must be undertaken.

The type of organization and its culture, norms, systems, and structures dramatically affect the pace of team development. Although established cultures may be burdened with traditions, they can still experiment. They have the luxury of sponsoring a protected pilot project using teams that can try out new relationships and duties while the rest of the organization runs in the traditional way. If the experiment is a success, the team concept can be moved out of the laboratory and its most successful elements can be implanted elsewhere.

At first glance, it would seem advantageous to implement teams in start-ups rather than in existing operations. Start-ups have no baggage to tote—no years of neglect; no established, older work force; no antagonistic unions; and no policies and procedures fixed in concrete. But start-ups come with their own set of problems. All at once, workers are asked to master complex new technologies; to adopt new, more flexible work rules; and to learn the more ambiguous but equally important skills of working participatively in a team. There is no sense of history, no shared vision or values—and suddenly there is too much to do. In the organizational world, few things are more hectic than start-up situations.

On the other side of the coin, implementing teams in existing organizations can have benefits. You are working with known quantities and are not burdened with the tremendous pressure that accompanies the opening of a new facility; on the other hand, you usually have less latitude in terms of people and policy changes.

Whatever the case, whether you are dealing with a start-up or a retrofit of an existing operation, it is best to proceed slowly, touching all the bases, making sure that the change is carefully managed, and assuring that teams have a secure root system from which to grow. When self-directed teams are linked to a sound business strategy, they have a solid foundation; like any other business initiative, they must be properly funded, carefully nurtured, measured, and rewarded. Your teams will make mistakes and, with the appropriate support, will adapt, adjust, and finally prosper.

## TEAM TIPS

Deciding where and when to implement teams can be a tricky endeavor. Here are some guidelines to follow as you embark on the journey.

## Don't Use a Cookbook Approach

Team implementations vary from organization to organization and, within an organization, from unit to unit. Teams even differ in terms of their size, the degree of responsibility they take on, and the role of the leader. It may be tempting to re-create the same design you have seen on one of your site visits or heard about at some conference. Yes, you should learn from the mistakes and successes of others. But it is also important for your attempt at teams to take into account your business needs, culture, and organizational vision.

The same advice applies to the approach you use to design teams. We are aware of dozens of organizations that specialize in team design. Each has a slightly (or in some cases radically) different approach to the steps and processes it uses to design teams. There is no single right way to go about the design process. In this chapter we have attempted to outline only some of the key features and guidelines we have found to be common in the majority of team implementations.

## Don't Abdicate Responsibility

Throughout this chapter, we have encouraged heavy involvement of all stakeholders in the team design process. We believe that widespread involvement increases commitment not only to the team approach but also to the quality of the implementation.

At the same time, converting to teams does require clarity in terms of both direction and roles. It is the responsibility of senior management and/or the steering committee to communicate the team vision, clarify who is responsible for each element in the design process, and share any limitations or boundaries that will affect the way teams operate.

## Be Willing to Accept Help

In our opinion, team design is a combination of experience, skill, and good judgment. If you have never gone through a design process, we recommend that you rely on some help to get you started. In many organizations—Digital Equipment Corporation in Enfield, Connecticut, for example—internal facilitators are available to help speed and guide team implementation. If such help is not available, outside organizations can assist you through the design process.

At the same time, keep in mind the first lesson: Don't use a cookbook approach to team design. The internal team champions, as well as the steering committee and design team, should make most of the decisions about what is "right" for your organization. The role of an internal or external resource is more that of a process facilitator than an expert.

## If You Start, Finish

One manager leading a team change effort in his company has a sign in his office that reads "Backing Up Causes Severe Tire Damage." As discussed in the previous chapter, it is best to assess your readiness for teams carefully before you start the implementation. However, once you *do* give the nod, be prepared to devote the resources and time you will need to see the installation through. We have found that to some degree, empowerment is addicting. Once your teams begin to feel some of the excitement and challenge of ownership, most team members will want more. While the going may get tough, backing up (or pulling out) of the implementation process can make it difficult ever to get things going again.

The team design process is a critical step in any team implementation. Dozens of organizations are leaping into team conversions without thinking through the hundreds of key issues that will face them later down the road. Those "leaders" are in for either a rough ride or a bad accident. Going through a design process not only ensures getting off to a good start but also helps to build the commitment of those who will be affected by the change.

## Provide Necessary Limits to the Design

We know one organization that gave its design team the assignment of recommending an "appropriate compensation system." Management had in mind some sort of pay-for-skill system, but they didn't adequately convey this information to the team. After six months of work, the design team presented a complete revision of the organization's performance management and compensation systems that senior management couldn't accept. The design team became demoralized, and the implementation was set back by a year.

The moral is that limits, boundaries, and expectations should be thought out carefully and communicated in advance. In general, it is better to loosen these limits gradually than to suddenly "change the rules."

# 7

# THE NEW LOOK OF LEADERSHIP:

## What's Left for a Leader to Do?

A s explained in Chapter Two, empowered teams eventually take on many of the responsibilities traditionally reserved for managers and supervisors. These include hiring new team members, scheduling work, ensuring quality, negotiating vendor relationships, and purchasing equipment.

As teams assume more responsibility, the roles of the first-line supervisor and other managers change, sometimes radically. As one might imagine, such a change often elicits fear, anger, ambiguity, and resistance. For many it is not an easy transition to make. After all, we have been taught that leadership is reserved for the "elite" few and that the leaders of our organizations make the difference, not the people on the floor or in the back office. Just look at the dozens of books written in the past decade that have exalted leadership. We spend our entire careers trying to climb *up* the organizational ladder—not *down*. As Ralph Stayer, CEO of Johnsonville Foods, put it, ". . . the very things that brought me success—my centralized control, my aggressive behavior, my authoritarian business practices—were creating the environment that made me so unhappy. If I wanted to improve results, I had to increase their [employees'] involvement in the business" (Stayer, 1990, p. 67).

One can't help but ask the question: If teams begin to manage themselves, what is left for the leader to do? In this chapter, we review in more detail the changing role of leadership, explore ways to make the transition as smooth as possible, and discuss some special issues facing leaders in an empowered environment.

## CHANGING ROLES

All organizations face the challenge of changing leadership roles as they implement empowered teams. As Fred Emery wrote, "The role of the foreman is so central to the traditional authoritarian system, that the first question to ask of any proposed scheme for democratization of work is, 'What does it do to the foreman's role?' If it leaves that role intact, then the scheme is fraudulent" (Emery, 1980, p. 21).

Today, more than a decade after Emery's article, most organizations on the road to empowerment still deal with this key issue. Numerous models present a new look at expectations and roles for leaders in organizations that are moving toward teams and empowerment. One of the more interesting of these models has been developed by Manz and Sims (1989). In their eyes, effective leaders, or "superleaders" as the authors call them, "lead others to lead themselves." Some of the behaviors they propose that leaders teach members include setting goals for one's own work efforts, practicing work activities through mental or physical rehearsal before performing them, and observing and gathering data about one's own performance. The key here is that superleaders encourage and coach others to internalize and self-manage much of the "control" that was previously imposed by supervisors and managers.

Jessup (1990) presents three "hats" that leaders, regardless of their title, must wear in team-based organizations: administrator, coach, and adviser. The administrator helps the team to meet its objectives through goal setting, problem solving, and other group processes. The coach focuses on helping the team develop as it matures. According to Jessup, the "job of the coach is to eventually eliminate the coach" (p. 81). The adviser provides the team with the necessary technical support, being careful to convey the skills and knowledge team members need to make their own decisions.

The Becton, Dickinson and Company plant in Durham, North Carolina, used a pie chart (Figure 7.1) during its team transition to show how leadership responsibilities would change over time. Note that the major increase is a shift *away* from control and *toward* coaching. Similarly, Howmet Corporation's Wichita Falls casting division worked with supervisors over a two-year period to make the gradual transition from employee involvement to a concept called "work cells"—in essence, teams that are organized around products (Echols and Mitchell, 1990). Figure 7.2 lists some of the specific responsibilities expected of Howmet's cell supervisors (a title they retain) as they began to share leadership responsibilities with their cell members.

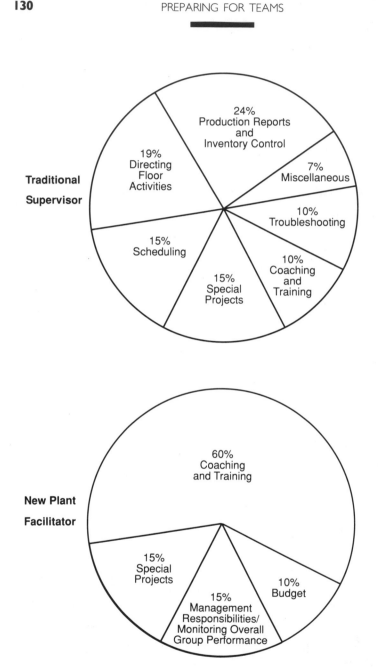

**Figure 7.1.** Changing role of the supervisor at Becton, Dickinson and Company. Reprinted courtesy of Becton, Dickinson and Company.

**Just-In-Time**
- Develop expertise in waste-free manufacturing.
- Teach operators the cell concept and basics of one-piece flow.
- Work with operators to refine cell layout, design, and functioning.
- Acquire technical knowledge of all cell processes and operations.
- Keep management informed of cell progress.

**Training**
- Identify cell training needs, both job related and interpersonal.
- Work with the cell to develop a cross-training plan.
- See that cell members are properly trained in needed technical skills.
- Coach cell members in performing aspects of your job that are handed off.

**Team Dynamics**
- Assist cell members in solving problems they confront.
- Counsel cell members when interpersonal conflict occurs.
- Get cell members to examine how they are working together.
- Provide helpful and constructive feedback to the cell.
- Help build teamwork among cell members and those groups with which the cell interacts.

**Traditional Tasks**
- See that schedule changes are made.
- Make sure the cell has the resources it needs to get the job done right.
- Interface with technical staff to ensure proper support.
- Handle disciplinary situations as appropriate.
- See that paperwork is completed.

**Self-Leadership**
- Coach cells to function in your absence.
- Develop the self-leadership capabilities of cell members.
- Help cells make decisions for themselves.
- Help cells become as self-sufficient as possible.

**Figure 7.2.** Specific responsibilities of Howmet Corporation's cell supervisors. Reprinted courtesy of Howmet Corporation.

# LEADERSHIP DIMENSIONS

Over the past several years, our own work with teams in the area of selection has enabled us to conduct in-depth job analyses with dozens of organizations that are moving toward the empowered team concept. The purpose of these analyses was to identify the dimensions (skills, knowledge, and motivations) required for effective leadership performance. We have performed these analyses for both team leader and group leader positions.

Our "working definition" holds that a team leader's position is *inside* the team. This position is usually held by a team member, and the responsibility may rotate among members over designated time periods. The term *group leader* refers to leadership positions *outside* the team (these positions also may be called *manager, coach,* or *facilitator*).

As teams assume more responsibilities, such as assigning tasks and coordinating and communicating with other departments, the group leader usually takes on new challenges. These might include operating in a larger organizational arena and assuming many functions previously performed by middle managers. For example, as teams move up the empowerment continuum, operational planning may become less important, while strategic planning may increase in importance.

Following is a list of dimensions for the position of group leader. These dimensions may change in importance, or certain dimensions may be replaced by others, as teams become more self-sufficient.

### Group Leader Dimensions

Ability to Learn (Applied
　　Learning)

Analysis (Problem Identification)

Business Planning

Collaboration

Communication (Oral and Written)

Delegation of Authority and
    Responsibility

Developing Organizational
    Talent

Follow-up

Individual Leadership
    (Influence)

Information Monitoring

Initiative

Judgment (Problem Solution)

Maximizing Performance

Meeting Leadership

Motivation to Empower Others

Operational Planning

Organizational Fit (Compatibility
    of Personal Values with
    Values of the Organization)

Rapport Building

Work Standards

## CLARIFYING RESPONSIBILITIES

With changes in the roles of the leaders in team organizations, "controllers," "planners," and "inspectors" are replaced with "coaches," "facilitators," and "supporters." As can be imagined, the downward migration of leadership responsibilities within the organization, coupled with the new role that leaders are asked to assume, can cause considerable role-clarity problems for both leaders and team members.

Some organizations initially keep the roles of the team and the leader unclear, letting them evolve at their own pace; they don't want to interfere with the evolution of their teams. More commonly, however, organizations have a vision of where they want their teams to end up, and they establish benchmarks along the way.

To accomplish this goal, it is important for leaders to have clearly defined roles relative to those of the team, and vice versa. Such a *role contract* does not have to impose rigid role boundaries; role changes can emerge through mutual consent. But with a role contract, leaders will not be surprised when the team assumes responsibility for roles that previously were theirs.

Some organizations provide explicit role expectations for different phases of team development. One organization planned to involve leaders in all team functions during the first year of team operation, then gradually diminish the leaders' involvement. The entire plan for "weaning," including the setting of monthly goals, was worked out in advance.

As teams progress along the empowerment continuum, the leader's role with the teams shifts from direct to indirect involvement. During this period, it is important to provide leaders with new responsibilities to replace those that have shifted to the team. The leader might be assigned more teams to coach or might take on a portion of the responsibilities formerly held by higher management.

There are a number of ways to help establish clarity among the roles of the teams, the team leaders, and the leaders and support staff outside the team. Many organizations hold frequent *role-clarity sessions* for the team leader, group leader, and team members during the early phases of team implementation. In these meetings team leaders, group leaders, and team members negotiate the functions for which they will be responsible, as well as the methods of measuring success in each function. Overlaps in perceived responsibilities surface, and functions that might have fallen between the cracks are identified.

Other organizations use a similar method called *responsibility charting*. As shown in Figure 7.3, the group leader, team leader, and team members work together to list their responsibilities and then decide who handles each one by assigning codes or checkmarks to the chart. This process should be used frequently at first while teams are learning to handle more leadership responsibility.

## SPECIAL LEADERSHIP ISSUES

The following five points should be addressed as you consider the roles of team and group leaders within your organization.

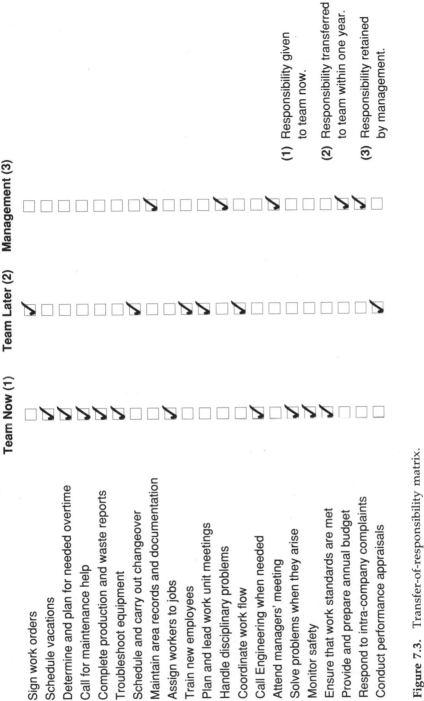

**Figure 7.3.** Transfer-of-responsibility matrix.

## Tenure and Replacement of Team Leaders

Tenure and replacement of team leaders are key issues among organizations that use self-directed teams. Fifty-one percent of the organizations responding to the Survey reported some form of team leader rotation. Of this 51 percent, the majority were chosen by election and the remainder by such methods as management appointment and seniority. The remaining 49 percent of the Survey organizations appear to have "permanent" team leaders.

Length of rotation varies among organizations and can range from three months to a year. The obvious advantage to rotation is that it reinforces the concept of shared leadership by giving every team member a valuable developmental opportunity. Schreiber Foods, for example, believes that rotation sensitizes members to the problems of the team leader and makes them more supportive of their leader's decisions.

Leadership rotation, however, can have its problems. It can place people in positions where they feel uncomfortable or unsure of themselves and sometimes can lead to poor performance. Some people are effective contributors but do not want to assume leadership responsibility; others may not have the skills to do so.

One organization we worked with experienced an additional problem: continuity. Some team leaders were hesitant to tackle longer-term and more complex issues because they knew that they would not be in the team leader position long enough to see those issues through to resolution.

## Sources of Candidates for Team Leader Positions

Most team leader positions are filled from within the ranks of the team. In the case of more permanent positions, the question might arise: "Wouldn't this policy penalize a highly qualified individual who happens to be on a team that doesn't presently need a leader?'' Meanwhile, another less qualified person might get a position through a chance opening on his or her team.

In order to address this concern, some organizations open permanent team leader positions to members of other teams. The selection decision is then made by members of the team that has the open position, by management, or by representatives from several teams.

## Tenure and Replacement of Group Leaders

In almost all cases, group leader and management positions in organizations with empowered teams are permanent positions. They usually are filled from the ranks of team leaders, and the selection decisions are frequently made by upper management.

It is becoming more common, however, for management to seek the advice of team members in making these selection decisions. In two organizations we work with, the teams actually were asked to play an active role in selecting new plant managers.

## Team Leader and Group Leader Performance Evaluations

Team and group leaders usually are appraised by managers ''above'' them, as well as by their team members. Many teams use some kind of instrument by which team members periodically evaluate team performance, cohesiveness, and efficiency. Leaders obtain indirect (and sometimes direct) feedback on their own effectiveness from such measurement tools. For example, a leader might gain insight on how well he or she is facilitating team cohesiveness. For the most part, these instruments are used for self-improvement and not for salary or other administrative purposes.

In developing a leader performance appraisal system, it is important to focus on both the "what" and the "how." The "what" consists of specific, measurable performance objectives or goals in areas such as quality, productivity, efficiency, and service. The "how" comprises the behavioral dimensions that facilitate job performance, such as coaching, communication, and influence. These dimensions are critical to setting the foundation of the new leadership role.

## Compensation of Team Leaders

Most organizations provide special remuneration for team leaders. The most common plan involves an hourly differential pay of fifty cents to one dollar per hour for the team leader. In some organizations, this differential increases with the team leader's experience. For example, during the first year, a leader might receive a differential of fifty cents per hour, the second year seventy-five cents, and the third year one dollar. Such a plan communicates the expectation that an individual will serve as a team leader for an extended period of time. Of course, in organizations that expect frequent changes in the team leader position, a compensation system that rewards tenure is inappropriate.

One Midwest manufacturing company that recently moved toward teams purposely kept the salary differential low. The company's thinking? It wanted dedicated people in the position who were interested in being team leaders for reasons other than the added compensation involved.

## TEAM TIPS

We have learned several lessons that should be helpful to you in your own move toward changing leadership roles. Following are our recommendations.

## Involve Managers and Supervisors in the Change Process

Moving supervisors and managers into new roles is best done *with* them rather than *to* them. They often are involved in the steering committees and design teams (see Chapter Six) that help get work teams started. Early involvement can be a key to success. Supervisors and managers not only need to be part of the change; they also need to be part of the vision. They can play a valuable role in helping teams through the "bumps and bruises" in the early stages of development. These people also have considerable content knowledge and technical skills that can prove invaluable to both the team and the organization.

Adolph Coors Company's brewery warehouse operation firmly believed that the team concept did not mean doing away with leadership. As a result, it relied heavily on supervisors to create empowered work teams. In essence, these supervisors led the change. Similarly, Howmet's Wichita Falls casting division involved supervisors extensively in its work cell redesign process.

## Provide Leadership Support and Training

Many leaders who have weathered the transition successfully complain not about the team concept but about the way it was introduced. In almost any team conversion, supervisors and managers have their egos and security on the line. To survive, they must master a whole new role in the organization.

Every effort should be made to retain the same group of leaders while going through the change process. Emotional support and coaching are a must. Coors, for example, encouraged "Straight Talk" sessions in which supervisors got together to openly share issues, concerns, and fears about their role changes.

As will be discussed in Chapter Nine, training is also a key to successful transition. We mentioned earlier that you are not only teaching new skills, but you are also trying to break down years of preconceived notions about effective leadership. Training should focus on new leadership skills, the nature of teamwork, workplace redesign, and the "ins" and "outs" of the self-directed team concept.

## Recognize and Reward Leadership That Encourages Teamwork and Empowerment

Organizational systems (and senior management) must facilitate the change process, not hinder it. If the organization insists on numerous controls, rewards managers for individual rather than team performance, shows little patience, and possesses no tolerance for mistakes, then strong "caution" signals are sent to the new team and group leaders.

Behaviors that involve "letting go" and "handing over" should be rewarded and recognized. One of this book's authors recently visited an automobile parts plant at the same time as the plant's corporate senior staff was being shown around. The vice-president of manufacturing seemed irritated that the plant manager did not have a host of up-to-the-minute production data at his fingertips. The manager had decided to let the teams collect and monitor these data while keeping him informed on a periodic basis. The message sent was, "You're not on top of your job." The message *should* have been, "Hey, things here are humming—good job in helping your teams become more accountable for those figures."

## Have Realistic Expectations About the Pace of Change

In our view, the majority of organizations expect too much too soon. Conversely, a handful of them make the change process take longer than is needed. Teams are more than an intervention—

they change the way work is performed and managed. It is also important to keep in mind that new leadership skills and behaviors are not developed overnight.

A new Motorola plant in Texas that is about to start a transition to teams expects the role of the supervisor to change over a four- to five-year period. Howmet Corporation has been working with its supervisors on a gradual transition to work cells for two years.

## Delegate Responsibility When Teams Are Ready

Leaders should pace their rate of change to that of the team. They can sometimes "let go" too quickly, before teams are ready to handle all the tasks required of a self-directed team. Coaching teams to success does not mean abdicating all responsibility. Constant reference to a delegation matrix or some other tool can help leaders and teams gauge the pace of change.

The famous sixth-century B.C. Chinese philosopher Lao-Tzu described the role of the leader more than twenty-four centuries ago: "A leader is best when people barely know he exists, not so good when people obey and acclaim him, worse when they despise him. . . . But of a good leader, who talks little, when his work is done, his aim fulfilled, they will say: We did this ourselves."

In effect, Lao-Tzu accurately described empowered leadership. This new leadership role can be rewarding for team members and leaders alike. As one leader in a North Carolina plant put it, "I really feel good because now I can work on the long-range planning and problem-solving areas in which I can make a contribution. I'm not bothered every five minutes by someone wanting me to make a decision when they know the right answers already" (Jessup, 1990). Similarly, a supervisor at a Motorola warehouse stated, "I enjoy the team concept. I have less responsibility and stress than before. People who *should* have the responsibility *do.*"

Even at the senior level, Robert Hass, Levi Strauss's CEO, stated, "It has been difficult for me to accept the fact that I don't have to be the smartest guy on the block. . . . In reality, the more you establish parameters and encourage people to take initiatives within those boundaries, the more you multiply your own effectiveness by the effectiveness of other people" (Howard, 1990, p. 135).

CHAPTER

8

# SELECTING TEAM PLAYERS:
## Choosing the Right People for Teamwork

A ny good coach in the sports field knows that it's a lot easier to build a winning team with skilled and motivated players. The same is true of self-directed work teams.

Careful selection is important in a start-up operation or in the conversion of an existing facility. In a start-up situation, people at all levels—from senior management to team member—can be assessed for the skills and motivation required for them to work in an empowered team atmosphere. For existing facilities making a conversion, selection can occur over a period of time as different areas of the operation convert to teams. Individuals who do not seem to be good team player prospects can be placed in more traditional settings, while those who have a higher probability of team success can be selected for empowered teams.

As turnover occurs, new team members can be selected based on their capabilities, skills, and motivation to work in a team environment. Promotion decisions also can be made by using more advanced selection technology.

Many teams have discovered that good selection is a critical and often irreversible part of the process. If the team is inadvertently stacked with dysfunctional members, it will be difficult to change their behavior or remove them from the team without disrupting the cohesiveness of the team.

In one organization we worked with, we saw a team of data processing professionals coping with one member who was not pulling her fair share of the work load. This team member's lack of initiative caused extra work for the others and forced them to confront a behavior problem before they were capable of handling it constructively. Eventually, after a string of unpleasant interactions, the member who was not contributing was asked to leave—but not before one of the other team members quit and the leader asked to be transferred. Careful selection of team members can prevent such casualties.

This chapter contains an overview of the methodology, systems, and issues we have found to be important in helping more than 100 organizations select the team members, team leaders, group leaders, and management for empowered team environments. A series of monographs is available for those readers who wish to learn more about developing such selection systems in their organizations (Byham, 1987, 1990; Hauenstein and Byham, 1989).

# JOB ANALYSIS

The first step in setting up a good selection process is to carefully define the criteria for job success by using some form of *job analysis*. A job analysis generates a list of the behaviors, technical knowledge, skills, and motivational areas that differentiate between successful and unsuccessful performers. A good analysis establishes a clearly defined set of job requirements or selection targets called *dimensions* against which candidates can be compared. A dimension is a description under which specific behavior, knowledge, or motivational elements that are associated with job success can be classified reliably.

Organizations that do not have an accurate list of well-defined job dimensions will waste time and effort evaluating the wrong attributes of applicants, often including elements related to gender, race, or national origin that are not job related. This causes inaccurate decisions and risks Equal Employment Opportunity problems. Dimensions defined through a job analysis give focus to the selection process.

If a selection system is being developed for an up-and-running organization, the job analysis procedure is relatively straightforward. Job incumbents are interviewed about their job activities and challenges, and higher-level personnel are interviewed about the perceived differences between effective and ineffective performers. In the latter situation, called a "critical incident discussion," people who are knowledgeable about the target job describe situations that are typical of successful and unsuccessful incumbents. In large-scale job analyses, the interview data are supplemented with questionnaire responses and occasionally with direct job observation.

When an organization is initiating a team structure for the first time, model jobs on which to base the job analysis are not available. In this case, it is best to call together a group of people

## SAMPLE DIMENSION: TEAMWORK

The Teamwork dimension is defined as "active participation in, and facilitation of, team effectiveness; taking actions that demonstrate consideration for the feelings and needs of others; being aware of the effect of one's behaviors on others."

Active cooperation by every member is vital to team success. Team members cannot sit back and observe or allow others to do the work; they must work proactively to achieve group goals and facilitate cohesiveness.

Effective teams are not just collections of people. Rather, they comprise an entity that is greater than the sum of its parts. This means that team members must work together closely and make every effort to cooperate with and support one another.

Key behaviors of the Teamwork dimension include the following:

- Asking for ideas

- Offering help without being asked

- Accepting suggestions

- Taking into consideration the needs, motivations, and skills of other team members when offering help or advice

- Working with other team members to solve a problem

- Recognizing and considering others' ideas

who have expertise in the technical requirements of the new operation and who also have the vision of the new culture and value system. Through a series of "visioning" exercises, this group can make informed decisions about the required job dimensions. Members of the steering committee or design team would be a natural source of participants for such a meeting.

The critical behaviors that are mentioned most frequently by team members, team leaders, and design committee members are interpersonal in nature. In job analysis interviews, we often hear experienced team leaders and members remark, "I'll take someone with a good attitude over someone with just technical skills any day. I can *train* technical skills." With further probing, we usually discover that they are really talking about interpersonal skills. Effective team members willingly pitch in, support and encourage others, volunteer to work on problems, and avoid adversarial "me-against-you" situations. Because these qualities can be difficult to detect in a casual selection process, they often are overlooked in the pursuit of apparent, more objectively measured technical skills.

The output from a job analysis process not only serves as the foundation of a good selection system but also helps to guide the development of training plans and appraisal systems as well as other human resource systems. For example, many team-oriented organizations develop their team training programs around dimensions that are defined through job analyses. Others make the job analysis dimensions part of their team-based performance appraisal system.

## TEAM MEMBER ASSESSMENT

Most organizations make their hiring decisions based on application forms, unstructured interviews, and reference checks. The most common technique is the interview, yet many critical requirements for effective team membership are not assessed easily in an interview—especially since the majority of interviews are poorly conducted.

Interviews tend to work best when the applicant has had experience in the type of job for which he or she is being interviewed. Unfortunately, many applicants for team positions have had no experience working in teams, so it can be difficult to estimate in interviews how effective a prospect will be when placed in a team position.

Faced with this problem, many team-oriented facilities have borrowed a technique from managerial or supervisory selection—the *assessment center* method. In an assessment center, candidates go through a series of simulations that mirror job-related activities, while people trained in observation evaluate their performance. Over the last five years, this methodology has been applied extensively to choosing work team members.

Team member assessment processes typically include two or three simulations that enable candidates to demonstrate their skills in situations similar to the team tasks they will perform on the job. Some typical simulations for team members include problem-solving, manufacturing, and group discussion exercises.

## Problem-Solving Simulations

Problem-solving exercises typically consist of fact-finding and decision-making simulations. The applicant is given a brief description of the circumstances concerning a production or service problem. The task is to seek information and make a decision regarding the problem within a limited period of time. During the fact-finding phase, the applicant may obtain additional information by questioning a resource person. At the conclusion of the fact-finding phase, the applicant makes a series of decisions. The resource person may question the applicant to probe his or her quality of reasoning. I/N Tek used an exercise such as this to help select people from Inland's traditionally managed Harbor Works operation for its new mill.

## Manufacturing Simulations

In one version of this group exercise, applicants are placed in the role of team members of a small parts-assembly firm. Jobs within the team are self-assigned, and the team must make key decisions regarding planning and allocating resources. Subaru-Isuzu used this type of exercise to help select associates for its start-up. This type of simulation is ideal for assessing learning ability, teamwork, problem solving, and work pace or tempo.

## Group Discussion Simulations

Group discussion exercises usually involve leaderless group discussions with nonassigned roles. Four short case studies of typical problems faced by team members are presented to a group of three to six applicants. These individuals are asked to make decisions about problems involving productivity, disputes among fellow team members, worker-safety problems, and tardiness. They submit consensus recommendations for each. The exercise assesses judgment, communication skills, teamwork, and leadership. Colgate-Palmolive used such a group discussion exercise to help staff a facility in Cambridge, Ohio.

These types of simulations, with modification, have been used in a wide range of manufacturing industries and service organizations. In addition to simulations, organizations may employ several other techniques to ensure selection of the most suitable candidates.

## Application Form

Applicants interested in team member positions usually complete an application form. We recommend structuring these forms around the key dimensions identified in the job analysis.

## Video Orientation

Often, groups of applicants are asked to watch an orientation video that realistically portrays what it would be like to work in the new team environment. The video also previews the upcoming selection system. The purpose of the orientation video is twofold: First, those who like what they see will be highly motivated to continue in the selection process. Second, those who do not like what they see will *self-select out* of the applicant pool. Videos have been used by team-based organizations such as Toyota in Georgetown, Kentucky, and Valeo Engine Cooling in Greensburg, Indiana.

## Cognitive Ability Test

A cognitive ability test assesses basic judgment, perception, and psychomotor skills. It can provide an accurate indication of whether candidates have the necessary ability to learn the changing technical aspects of the job.

## Self-Report Inventory

Many organizations use some sort of self-report inventory designed to assess the extent to which the tasks and responsibilities inherent in a team environment match the applicant's motivations. Motivations such as collaboration, internal work standards, the desire to learn, and the desire to generate and take responsibility for ideas are assessed in such an instrument.

Here are sample items from a validated instrument we developed for team selection called the Job Fit Inventory. For each statement, the applicant indicates on a five-point scale the degree to which he or she agrees or disagrees.

- Managers and employees can solve problems by talking to each other.

- It doesn't matter whether I feel I'm contributing to the progress of the organization as long as I get paid.

- Before beginning a new assignment, I like to get input from others.

- Asking people to switch jobs keeps them from improving their work skills.

- Workers and management must cooperate to maximize productivity.

- Job safety is mainly the responsibility of the people who design the machines and buildings.

## Technical Skill Tests

Many times it is important to evaluate the technical skills of applicants to determine whether they can fill in at other skilled positions within the team when necessary. Usually a paper-and-pencil test is used as an initial screen; a hands-on observation of skill application is then used to make the final selection.

## Targeted Interviewing

As mentioned earlier, interviews are a key component of any selection system. Unfortunately, however, interviewers often obtain unimportant *theoretical data* about a candidate instead of *facts* about the candidate's actual past behavior. Theoretical data (answers to questions such as "What would you do differently if you were hired in our team-oriented company?") can lead to inaccurate predictions of an individual's potential for success on the job.

To avoid these problems, use the following four principles for improving the effectiveness of selection interviews:

1. Focus the interview only on information that is relevant to job-related dimensions. This will enable you to assess the applicant's likelihood for success in a specific job.

2. Direct the interview process toward obtaining specific behavioral examples of past experiences. Avoid asking questions that produce theoretical answers requiring interpretation, such as "How would you change your job?" instead of "What changes have you recommended in your present job?"

3. Apply effective interviewing techniques. Effective interviews include asking behavioral rather than theoretical questions, maintaining the applicant's self-esteem, and learning to ask specific follow-up questions that evoke concrete answers.

4. Involve several interviewers in organized data exchange discussions. In most cases, more than one person should be involved in the assessment process so that they can share information on applicants in a systematic fashion. Each dimension should be evaluated prior to reaching consensus on a hiring decision.

Once you have determined which selection techniques best match the dimensions that were revealed in your job analysis, it is a good idea to develop a matrix or grid, as shown in Figure 8.1. An "X" indicates that the dimension on the left side of the grid is being "assessed" by the selection technique given on the top of the grid. The dimension selection grid matches the selection techniques to the dimension, ensuring appropriate coverage of each dimension in the system. The grid also helps to prevent unnecessary overlap (for example, four people interviewing for the same dimension). The grid shown in Figure 8.1 is based on a team member selection process.

## TEAM AND GROUP LEADER SELECTION

In shifting to the team concept, most organizations choose to identify or select their leaders (managers, group leaders, and team leaders) before selecting the team members. This makes sense since

**Assessment Instruments**

| Dimensions | General Ability Test | Job Fit Inventory | Production Simulation | Problem-Solving Simulation | Team Discussion Simulation | Coaching Simulation | Reference Check | Job Interview (Team Member) | Job Interview (Staff Member) | Health Examination | On-the-Job Review |
|---|---|---|---|---|---|---|---|---|---|---|---|
| Ability to Learn | X | | | | | | | X | | | X |
| Analysis | | | | X | X | | | X | | | X |
| Attention to Detail | | | X | | | | | X | X | | X |
| Initiative | | | | | | | | X | X | | X |
| Job Fit | | X | | | | | | X | X | | X |
| Judgment | | | | X | X | X | | X | | | X |
| Oral Communication | | | | X | X | X | | X | X | | X |
| Physical Health | | | | | | | | | | X | X |
| Planning and Organizing | | | X | | | | | X | | | X |
| Influence | | | | | X | | | | X | | X |
| Teamwork (Cooperation) | | | | | X | | X | | X | | X |
| Tolerance for Stress | | | X | X | X | | | X | X | | X |
| Work Standards | | | X | X | X | | X | | X | | X |
| Training/Coaching | | | | | | X | | | | | X |

| | |
|---|---|
| The design provides multiple measures of the most important dimensions. | Dimensions that are less amenable to development are covered more heavily in the selection process. |

**Figure 8.1.** Dimension selection grid.

# LEGAL CONSIDERATIONS

A major concern regarding any process or technique that is used to make employment decisions is whether that process or technique is valid and fair to legally protected classes such as members of various ethnic groups, women, and persons with disabilities. Tests, interviews, background information, application blanks, and assessment center procedures all must be used in ways that will avoid or minimize adverse impact on the employment of protected groups.

One critical step is the validation process, which demonstrates that each selection methodology is job related for the team situation. Initially, this can be done successfully through a careful job analysis and selection of methodology. The job analysis shows that the assessed behaviors, knowledge, and motivations (the dimensions) describe the required on-the-job behaviors, knowledge, and motivations. The job analysis also shows that the tests and simulations are an appropriate sample of the work of a team member.

To ensure legal defensibility:

- The dimensions should be job related and carefully defined.

- The elements of the selection system must bring out behavioral knowledge and motivations that are related to the requirements of the target position.

- The evaluators (assessors) for each element must be trained in their roles in the assessment process and taught how to make reliable judgments.

- The data must be integrated in a systematic way by people who know the target job and understand the elements of the system, the dimensions, and the rating scale.

- *All* candidates must go through the same system.

In addition, an organization should establish an applicant tracking system to monitor the potential adverse impact of each element in the selection process. After the system is installed and working, the organization should conduct a criterion-related validity study to further document the system's accuracy.

these leaders are often responsible for the technical training of new team members, as well as for other start-up or transition activities.

Unfortunately, one of the most common regrets expressed to us in retrospect by the organizations we work with, especially in start-up situations, is that they did not use a more rigorous selection process in choosing their leaders. Too often senior managers either think that they instinctively know who will make an empowering leader or believe that the leader's technical and organizational expertise is more important than other job-related dimensions. They are often disappointed. Because leaders usually encounter the most stress, and therefore might be likely to revert to autocratic behaviors under pressure, we strongly recommend careful assessment of all leader candidates—starting at the top.

Leadership selection systems follow the same design principles as team member selection systems. However, since the dimensions vary, different selection instruments are used. For example, it is not unusual in a leadership selection system to see some type of coaching simulation that shows how well a leader will interact with a team member who has a proposal for quality improvement. Similarly, leaders may be put through complex business analyses and decision-making simulations.

# UNIQUE ASPECTS OF TEAM SELECTION

Approaches to team member selection differ from traditional selection practices in several significant ways.

## Team Members Are Often Involved in the Selection Process

Eighty-nine percent of the Survey respondents indicated that team members take part in the selection process. This usually means that members are trained in interview skills and participate in selecting candidates for their team. The most commonly reported advantage of this involvement is the team members' subsequent commitment to seeing that their candidates succeed. Fears that team members would "go easy on their friends" seem unfounded. In one case, at a specialty products manufacturer, a recently hired press team member drove back to the plant at eight o'clock one evening to tell the human resource support manager that one of his friends was applying for a job, but that he was "a whiner and complainer" and would not make a good team member.

## A Strong Effort Is Made to Provide a Realistic Job Preview

Early experiences with work teams showed that there was often a substantial amount of turnover within the first year of team start-up. One probable cause seemed to be that employees' expectations were not met. It appears that newly converted work team zealots may have oversold the opportunity, making it sound as if it were a once-in-a-lifetime chance to escape from authoritarian management practices. Those who enlisted were surprised to find that it was hard work and, in many ways, more stressful than their former jobs.

Since then, efforts have been made to present a more balanced picture of the job, often on videotape. A video depiction of the work also helps to excite the imaginations of candidates who have been beaten down by years of traditional management practices. It helps them visualize how teams really work.

## Different Criteria Are Used for Selection

Often the dimensions required for success as a team member differ from those that are traditionally used and recognized by management. Team member selection systems typically include dimensions such as initiative, teamwork, motivation and ability to learn, and the skills to influence others. If the culture does not truly reinforce and match the type of associates you are hiring, you are certain to frustrate and eventually lose them.

## The Selection Ratio Is Usually Large

In start-up operations, organizations commonly have encountered huge applicant pools relative to the number of openings available. For example, when Toyota opened a plant in Kentucky, it had more than 90,000 applicants for approximately 3,000 positions. The mean selection ratio of clients we work with is about 20 to 1—that is, companies assess twenty candidates for each one they hire.

Figure 8.2 shows a sample team member selection process. The system is designed with multiple "acceptance/rejection" points or hurdles represented by each block. The right side of the figure represents the percentage of candidates that would typically still be "in the system." For example, if 1,000 candidates applied for a job in Phase 1, the system would screen out about 800 upon completion of Phase 4. The selection techniques that can be administered on a "mass" basis and those that carry lower "per head" costs are positioned earlier in the selection process, increasing the system's efficiency.

Because of the volume of candidates and the intensity of the selection process, team-oriented organizations usually spend more time and money on selection than their more traditional counterparts. The cost per selected team member can range from $400 to $2,000. Invariably, this money is well spent. For instance, in one organization we conducted a *utility analysis,* a research method that calculates the return on investment of selection expenditures. For each dollar spent on selection, this analysis showed a return of over $100 in incremental improvements related to quality and productivity.

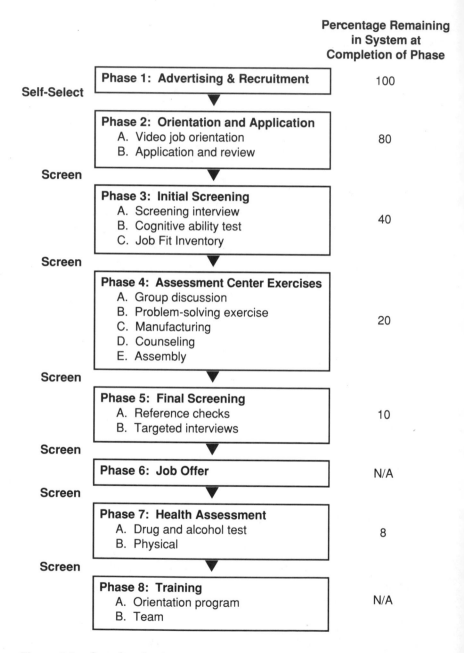

**Percentage Remaining in System at Completion of Phase**

**Self-Select**

**Phase 1: Advertising & Recruitment** — 100

**Screen**

**Phase 2: Orientation and Application**
A. Video job orientation
B. Application and review
— 80

**Screen**

**Phase 3: Initial Screening**
A. Screening interview
B. Cognitive ability test
C. Job Fit Inventory
— 40

**Screen**

**Phase 4: Assessment Center Exercises**
A. Group discussion
B. Problem-solving exercise
C. Manufacturing
D. Counseling
E. Assembly
— 20

**Screen**

**Phase 5: Final Screening**
A. Reference checks
B. Targeted interviews
— 10

**Screen**

**Phase 6: Job Offer** — N/A

**Screen**

**Phase 7: Health Assessment**
A. Drug and alcohol test
B. Physical
— 8

**Screen**

**Phase 8: Training**
A. Orientation program
B. Team
— N/A

**Figure 8.2.** Sample selection system.

# GUIDELINES FOR AN EFFECTIVE TEAM SELECTION SYSTEM

## Make It Accurate

- Base it on a job analysis in which behaviorally defined dimensions have been identified.
- Cover all dimensions within the selection system.
- Treat all applicants consistently.
- Be certain that each part of the system is valid.
- Use multiple evaluators (interviewers and assessors).
- Obtain information through multiple methods.
- Use systematic data integration.

## Make It Efficient

- Define rejection points throughout the system.
- Organize data about the job and organization (assuring that applicants have a complete understanding of the job).
- Organize a sequence of assessment phases (for example, place the least expensive techniques first).
- Make it adaptable for external hiring or internal promotion.
- Use dimensions as part of a complete personnel system.

## Document and Evaluate

- Document job analysis, evaluator training, and administration.
- Plan and conduct criterion-related research for validity.
- Plan and conduct research on any adverse impact on protected groups.
- Monitor administration (for example, use only trained evaluators).

## Train Your Organization's Representatives

- Provide training in selection system roles (provide specific written instructions).
- Train evaluators to make reliable judgments.
- Plan and conduct refresher training periodically.

## TEAM TIPS

The following three tips can help you successfully select team players for your organization.

## Schedule Applicants Appropriate to Needs

We have observed that many organizations wait too long to start the selection process. Then, under pressure to fill positions by a deadline, they lower their standards and take marginally qualified people. Bringing on team members too late also means losing critical orientation sessions, and training time also may be cut.

Conversely, we saw one organization start the selection process too early. They selected key team members ten months before they could get their hands on the new equipment. The high-initiative team members rapidly became bored with long weeks of classroom training and started to find new outlets for their initiative (not all of which were welcomed by management).

The optimum schedule for your operation will depend on your process and the amount of technical training needed. We have seen successful organizations bring the first people on board from two months to two years before opening.

## Don't Overselect for Your Needs

There can be various forms of inadvertent but deadly overselection. For example, when you select people with the intention of becoming a high-involvement organization but slip into old practices, you may end up with a group of people whose skills and motivations are unfulfilled. The consequences of such frustration are painful to observe and can lead to high turnover and aggravated labor problems.

Another way to overselect is to hire people who are overqualified or mismatched for the jobs they are asked to assume; this may result in early turnover and morale problems. For example, if organizations restrict job applicants to those who score in the top 1 percent of a cognitive ability test for production team members, they may find that they have a work force that can "think" but that is not motivated to work in a manufacturing environment. We have heard of start-up facilities that hired lawyers, accountants, and teachers for assembly jobs, then watched as these workers realized that assembly work was not for them. Our intention is not to put a value on different types of work; instead, we want to point out that job match and motivation as well as ability are essential for successful job performance.

## Be Sensitive to the Perceptions of the Community at Large

While more sophisticated selection systems are becoming common, there may be some side effects. Many organizations have reported positive effects similar to those described by Richard Walton at the pioneering Gaines dog food plant in Topeka, Kansas. Walton (1979) says, "This initial experience created a sense of hardiness, uniqueness and elitism among participants" (p. 424).

It is precisely this sense of elitism that, while helping to create cohesiveness among those selected, can tend to alienate the community at large. This problem is worsened by the unusually high selection ratios for most team-centered operations. If you are rejecting nineteen out of twenty applicants, you must have a plan to cope with a large number of disappointed people.

One effective approach embraced by many organizations is to show the value of open communication right from the beginning of the selection process. These organizations provide as much information as possible about the reasons behind the process, along with realistic estimates of candidates' likelihood of success. They make a special effort to demonstrate the job-relatedness of every part of the selection system, in some cases using videotapes to show how the selection techniques mirror job activities. They also couch all "rejections" in terms of "fit" with their unique culture and requirements to help prevent an unsuccessful candidate from losing self-esteem.

When open communication is provided and all elements of the selection system are clearly job related, organizations experience very few problems.

Teams *can* succeed without paying attention to selecting the right people. But it is worth the effort to make the right decisions up front because many skills and motivations are difficult to build or change later on. Empowered teams need the right combination of facilitative leadership and team-oriented associates to succeed, and well-designed selection is the first step toward achieving this goal.

CHAPTER

9

# TRAINING THE NEW TEAM:
## Planning and Supporting Critical Skill Development

When asked which factor most influences the success of teams, experienced practitioners invariably point to *training*. Not surprisingly, respondents to the Survey reported that inadequate training was the biggest hindrance to effective team performance.

Placing so much emphasis on training is understandable when you consider the specific types of skills members need in order to function effectively in a self-directed team. After all, people do not automatically possess these skills; past work environments may have reinforced habits contrary to those that are needed for successful teamwork. This is not a motivation problem; rather, people don't automatically know how to solve problems as a group, reach consensus decisions, or make presentations of ideas. Until their skills improve to the point where they feel comfortable, they will avoid performing these tasks at all costs. Fortunately, training for effective team performance *will* help, given enough time, planning, and resources.

Most training for teams can be organized into three categories: job skills, team/interactive skills, and quality/action skills.

*Job skills* encompass all the technical knowledge and skills team members need for success on the job. These may include operating a press, loading software, troubleshooting equipment, processing claims, and interpreting statistical process control charts. With empowered teams, these skills also can include knowledge of the organization's budgeting process, an understanding of its business, and the ability to make capital equipment requests. Multiskilling and skill-based pay systems make extensive job skills training critical for successful individual and team performance.

*Team/interactive skills* include all the interpersonal and communication skills team members need to be effective in their new roles. The team structure demands that these skills be considerably more sophisticated than in traditional operations. Some of the interactive skills required for team effectiveness include handling conflict, meeting leadership, negotiating requirements with suppliers and customers, and influencing others, particularly those in support functions.

*Quality/action skills* involve identifying problems and making improvements. In most teams, members are expected to take the initiative to make continuous improvements, whether this means suggesting ways to reduce cycle times or diagramming the causes of a particular nonconformance. Each member is a built-in team quality control expert.

Job skills, team/interactive skills, and quality/action skills have a multiplicative effect on one another. Imagine a team of six production technicians with strong job skills resulting from a total of ninety years on the job. This team has just completed a quality program and therefore has a strong quality focus, yet it has few or no team or interactive skills. Highs of 10 points in each category would produce a total of 1,000 (10 × 10 × 10). In our case, however, the total would be much less:

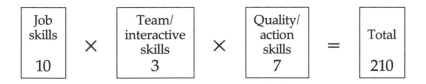

In this example, the team's efforts are drastically reduced by its inability to interact effectively. Just a slight increase—a few more points—in team/interactive or quality/action skills could easily double the team's effectiveness.

This is the sort of team that people find most annoying. One engineering support team we observed fit this profile. It managed to cause more headaches and complaints in its small manufacturing organization than all the other teams combined. This group tried to identify and solve problems (quality/action skills) and exercise its technical knowledge (job skills) by telling everyone else what they did wrong (absence of interactive skills). This caused a wide array of unproductive reactions. For instance, other teams no longer called, even if they needed engineering help. When they were forced to interact, members of other teams often deliberately disregarded the engineers' guidance.

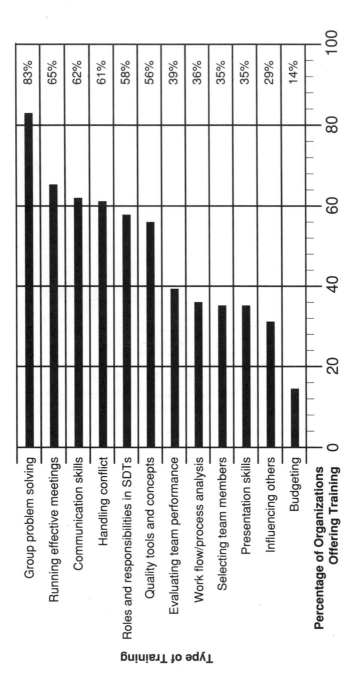

**Figure 9.1.** Kinds of team training delivered by organizations. Data extracted from Wellins, Wilson, Katz, Laughlin, and Day, 1990.

# INVESTING IN TRAINING

Near-disaster situations can be avoided by carefully considering *all* the skills your teams will need. The most logical starting place is a job analysis that identifies the job dimensions for team members' (or leaders') success (see Chapter Eight). Since these dimensions are based on the skills, knowledge, and abilities required for successful job performance, they can serve as content or curriculum areas around which to develop training. If you've used a dimensionally based selection process or have considered some sort of dimensional needs analysis, you will also have at your fingertips strengths and development needs for each team member or leader. These data can be the starting point in more effectively targeting training to individual needs.

Many team-based organizations devote large amounts of time to training. At Corning, for instance, team members spend 15 to 20 percent of their time in training—approximately one day a week. Aid Association for Lutherans has a two-year training program, starting with individuals and progressing to training for intact teams. Dana Corporation's employees were given forty hours of training over eighteen months when the company's valve plant converted to teams (Sheridan, 1990).

As a manager at Rohm & Haas's Kentucky chemical plant said, "The training load is enormous. Don't underestimate it or you'll end up always playing catch-up."

How do organizations structure their training time? The Survey revealed that organizations with self-directed teams provide a wide variety of training, as Figure 9.1 suggests. However, other than "group problem solving," training is by no means universal in many of these categories.

The Survey questions focused on broad skill areas. As mentioned earlier, a considerable amount of job-specific technical training usually is provided to ensure that jobs can be rotated among team members. This is especially true of pay-for-knowledge or pay-for-performance programs. A typical example is Chapparal Steel, where new team members receive technical skills training in the classroom four hours a week. This training is supplemented with an organized on-the-job training program that provides skill competency in all the jobs within a team's area.

Some organizations, like Johnsonville Foods, have adopted the philosophy of "learning by doing." For instance, when the plant needed a new production line, instead of farming out the design to engineers, the company gave the project to a group of team members. To redesign the line, team members had to learn about budgets, capital proposals, blueprints, and equipment costs. Their work proved to be an extremely effective learning experience because they were able to apply their new-found knowledge immediately on an actual project.

# PLANNING TRAINING FOR TEAM MEMBERS

There are a number of general principles or guidelines that should be considered when you develop and implement training for self-directed teams. Among them are two important principles:

1. A core set of skills must be provided to all associates while they are being organized into teams.

2. Ongoing training must be provided at the teachable moment.

## Providing a Core Set of Skills

As mentioned earlier, skills can be categorized into job skills, quality/action skills, and team/interaction skills. This section further breaks down the categories and describes core skills that our experience indicates are needed by all team members if they are to move along the empowerment continuum.

### Team/interaction skills

- *Listening and feedback.* Summarizing, checking for understanding, and giving and receiving constructive feedback

- *One-to-one communication.* Communicating with team members, customers, suppliers, and leaders

- *Handling conflict.* Identifying and resolving conflicts and disagreements within a team, with another team, or with a supplier or client

- *Influencing others.* Gaining the commitment or agreement of others

- *Training job skills.* Cross-training and coaching

- *Team skills (participating in meetings).* Developing roles and responsibilities, especially group process skills, of all participants in meetings

- *Working in teams.* Understanding the stages of team development and the factors needed for successful team performance (see Chapters Ten through Thirteen)

### Quality/action skills

- *Clarifying (internal and external) customer requirements.* Recognizing and defining customer needs

- *Identifying improvement opportunities.* Analyzing the root cause of any gap in meeting customer requirements

- *Developing and selecting solutions.* Creatively generating and sorting alternative solutions to problems

- *Planning the improvement.* Planning, monitoring, and measuring quality projects

- *Ensuring ongoing quality.* Standardizing improvements and identifying ongoing opportunities

### Job skills (highly job dependent)

- *Equipment operation.* Acquiring specific training in the operation of equipment production methods that are directly related to performing team jobs

- *Safety practices.* Following safety procedures and policies

- *Maintenance basics.* Learning basic machine preventive and total maintenance

- *Production processes.* Developing Just-In-Time systems and material requirements planning

We have found these skills to be the requirements for operating in an empowered team and for implementing constant improvement actions. Training in these core skills does not have to be delivered all at once; it can be spread out over months (and, in some cases, years). Its timing depends on the speed of the planned team empowerment.

These basic skills not only enhance team performance; they are also fundamental to empowerment. For example, it is not very empowering if a team member is required to go to a team leader or group leader every time there is a conflict within the team or with a support department. It is much more empowering if the individual has the skills and confidence to handle conflicts directly.

Planning quality improvements is another skill area that can affect empowerment. Interestingly, many team members become frustrated during early efforts to improve their areas of responsibility. They might have good ideas but experience obstacles in turning these ideas into actions. Skills that focus on planning and implementation can make the difference between the success or failure of an improvement idea.

## Providing Training at the Most Teachable Moment

Many of the core skills we have reviewed can be provided across the board early in a team implementation. However, other skills will need to be acquired by specific individuals or teams over time.

When you consider the total amount of training self-directed teams require, it is important to apply a Just-In-Time approach, where training is provided as close in time as possible to actual use of the skill. A great deal of training is rendered useless because the participants don't immediately have an opportunity to apply their newly learned skills. Training without good timing usually results in two reactions from participants: "Why am I in this training?" or (six months later) "Did we learn something about this . . . and where is that manual anyway?"

Presentation skills training is a good example of the importance of timing. Most self-directed team members will make presentations to managers, other teams, customers, suppliers, or others. Additionally, team members sometimes find themselves making presentations on their team efforts at professional conferences and symposia. Some organizations respond by providing a heavy dose of training in presentation skills as they start or convert to teams— when its value is not appreciated and its impact is diminished by the heavy load of other training provided at that time.

It is better to offer presentation skills training when those who are attending have immediate opportunities to apply what they have learned. Individuals who have an opportunity to apply a new skill are much more motivated to learn than those who lack that opportunity.

Some examples of Just-In-Time training opportunities are listed here:

- *Making presentations.* Preparing and delivering formal presentations to customers or managers

- *Leading meetings.* Developing leadership skills required for teams that are moving to shared leadership

- *Selecting team members.* Using targeted behavior-based interviewing and assessment skills

- *Assessing team performance.* Evaluating individual and team performance against established goals

- *Gaining team agreement.* Applying skills for group decision making and consensus building

Aside from the principle of the teachable moment, another good reason for a Just-In-Time approach is that not all team members need every advanced skill right away. For example, Subaru-Isuzu Automotive decided to involve team members in a progressive disciplinary process. The new system called for considerable training in both process and advanced feedback skills. However, since only a handful of associates would help manage this process, it was not essential to train every team member in these skills at once.

# LEADERSHIP TRAINING

Both team and group leaders usually require the same skills as team members. However, since these leaders will be making a transition to a coach or facilitator role, they will require additional skill building in areas such as encouraging initiative, coaching for success, reinforcing effective performance, overcoming resistance to change, managing conflict, and developing collaborative relationships.

Leaders are also expected to help the team manage its performance (especially in the early stages) and thus will need skills in areas such as performance appraisal and feedback, progressive discipline, and achieving commitment to goals. In addition, leaders are expected to deliver some of the team training. Thus, basic "platform skills," group facilitation skills, and the use of visual aids should be part of a leader's repertoire.

In making the transition to a new role, leaders often encounter a number of common problems:

- Some leaders tend to micromanage. In other words, they function in their old directive roles rather than in their new coaching roles.

- Some leaders avoid taking a strong stand on disciplinary action and other sensitive issues because they fear losing the respect and cooperation of team members.

- Some leaders may be afraid to empower because they do not trust their teams to produce the best possible solutions to problems.

- Some leaders do not know how to empower—that is, how to coach and offer help without taking responsibility for action.

Such problems are understandable and often relate to a lack of confidence or experience in handling a very different role. These problems can be overcome through a combination of training, time, and practice.

For example, some leaders initially will lack faith in a team's ability to solve its own problems, or they may be uncomfortable with their own effectiveness in handling ideas from subordinates.

What if a team member comes up with an idea that the leader thinks is flawed? If the leader expresses concern or vetoes the idea, the team might not offer ideas in the future. Leaders need the skills and confidence to handle new ideas in a way that maintains the motivation and commitment of both the individuals and the teams involved.

The skills of *situational delegation* and *situational control* are also important to leaders. These terms refer to situations in which certain teams, team leaders, or team members can be given more responsibility with less control because of the nature of the task or the history of the particular individuals and teams.

When leaders lack confidence, they are reluctant to face difficult performance or work habit situations. These leaders may avoid issues until they escalate into serious problems. Skill-based behavior modeling programs, coupled with on-the-job support and coaching, can help leaders develop the needed skills and the confidence to use them.

As with any good learning system, leadership training cannot be treated as a one-time event. Training should be continuous, particularly when the responsibilities of team leaders and group leaders change and their teams move up the empowerment continuum.

In organizations that use a rotating team leader position, or in cases where there is no formal team leader and all the team members share leadership responsibility, every team member needs to acquire team leadership skills.

## A Word About Coaching

Although the term "coaching" is used extensively in team environments, its actual practice frequently is misused since it takes a skilled leader to coach properly. Effective and empowering leaders encourage other leaders and members to solve problems on their own. They coach for success *before* the team member's action, not *after* the failure. Coaching for success increases the likelihood of success, which in turn builds confidence.

Coaching for success is a skill that can be developed. Leaders need to understand the critical steps in coaching, see a positive model of the steps being applied, and have an opportunity to practice and receive feedback. The key is to develop skills and confidence simultaneously during training.

Good coaches don't solve a team's problems; they help individuals solve *their own* problems. Coaches manage through questioning rather than dictating. Instead of effective coaches issuing orders, they ask, "What do you need to accomplish?" or "What alternatives have you considered?" or "Have you thought about how Maintenance is going to react to your idea?"

At no time does the leader take on the problem personally. Instead, by coaching individuals through the possible steps for handling the problem effectively, the leader offers help without taking responsibility for action. This is the soul of empowerment because it creates a sense of ownership. Out of habit, some team members want to give their problems to a leader to solve. Perhaps they lack the knowledge to solve a problem or don't have confidence in their own ability to solve it. The effective leader helps individuals and teams look at their problems and determine appropriate alternatives. Employees will feel empowered only if they solve problems themselves. Most importantly, the next time a problem comes up, they will be better able to deal with it.

As teams progress through the empowerment continuum, they expect their leaders to be more empowering and to coach the team to overcome obstacles, but not to do things for them. Coaches make themselves dispensable by developing *in others* the skills to handle problems.

## PLANNING TRAINING FOR THE
## SUPPORT TEAM MEMBER

Our experience is that support team members play a critical role in maintaining a high level of empowerment; therefore, we strongly recommend that support team members such as engineers, accountants, and purchasing agents complete a training plan similar to those used for team members and leaders. One "Attila the Hun" in an accounting support department, for example, can do more damage than any average misguided team leader.

Like effective leaders, effective support team members must grasp and practice the skills of empowerment, specifically by offering help without taking responsibility for action and by not solving problems for teams or team members. Support team members should help the teams or team members map out solutions to the problems so that they can solve the problems on their own. Such a role change can be difficult for support people because it sometimes calls for a drastic readjustment of the self-image these professionals hold. In most team organizations, however, the necessary adjustment is still compatible with their preferred image; that is, support departments find it easier to function as consultants than as dictatorial experts.

## SEQUENCING TRAINING

Another juggling act you will face is planning training over time in such a way that it effectively supports the development of team member and team leader skills. One organization we are acquainted with did a very effective job of planning its training as it started a small team-oriented line within a larger, more traditionally organized facility. Its plan, outlined in Table 9.1, contains several elements that are key to effective sequencing:

- Training stretches over several years.

- Training is sequenced in a logical order so that its various parts build on one another.

- Group leaders are trained in skills first, team leaders second, and team members third. This order enables the team and group leaders to act as trainers, provides them with an understanding of what their team members go through, and helps them see opportunities for coaching and reinforcement.

- Training is provided Just-In-Time where possible.

- Training in action skills is associated with real, on-the-job projects so that all participants can see an immediate application of their new skills.

- Activities involving team building and organization development activities are integrated into the training plan.

## MULTISKILLING AND CROSS-TRAINING

Throughout an organization's training plan, provisions must be made to schedule, support, and reinforce multiskilling and cross-training efforts. Multiskilling requirements lead to cross-training, which becomes a critical element in the health and development of teams.

In one complex chemical process operation, two employees performed their jobs for years without realizing that the actions of each directly affected the other's work. Although they worked physically close to each other and carried on long conversations, they never discussed the process. This resulted in an almost comical and never-ending chain of unnecessary adjustments. As one

**TABLE 9.1**

**Sequential Steps for Effective Team Training**

BEFORE TEAM START-UP

| Time Frame | Managers, Group Leaders, and Key Support Members | Team Leaders | Team Members |
|---|---|---|---|
| 12 months before | Facilitated agreement on mission, vision, and values for the line | (Not yet selected) | (Not yet selected) |
| 11 months before | Project planning and implementation training | | |
| 10 months before | Team-building activity<br>Management team development planning | | |
| 8 months before | Team-building activity | | |
| 6 months before | Selection skills training<br>Empowerment training<br>Leadership and influence training | | |
| 5 months before | Group leadership training | Orientation:<br>• Mission, vision, and values<br>• Role clarity<br>• Expectations and objectives<br>• Personal development planning<br>• Basic interaction skills training | |
| 4½ months before | Developing organizational talent training (to agree on development plans for team leaders) | | Technical training on new equipment and processes, interspersed with team-building activities |

| Time | Activity |
|---|---|
| 3 months before | Encouraging initiatives training (to help team leaders actually implement an improvement) | Action skills training:<br>• Analyzing customer requirements<br>• Identifying root causes<br>• Exploring alternatives<br>• Implementing improvements<br>• Evaluating projects |
| 2½ months before | —Joint Team-Building Activity— | |
| 2 months before | | Selection skills training |
| 1 month before | | Facilitator training:<br>• Coaching<br>• Reinforcing |
| 3 weeks before | | Job skills training | Orientation:<br>• Mission, vision, and values<br>• Expectations<br>• Personal development planning<br>• Basics of working in teams |
| 2 weeks before | | Leading meetings | Technical training on new equipment and processes, interspersed with basic interaction skills training |
| 1 week before | —Joint Team-Building Activity— | |

## TABLE 9.1 (Continued)

### AFTER TEAM START-UP

| Time Frame | Managers, Group Leaders, and Key Support Members | Team Leaders | Team Members |
|---|---|---|---|
| 5 weeks after | | Encouraging initiatives | Meetings skills: participating and leading |
| 6 weeks after | | (Team leaders deliver action skills training within their own teams) | Action skills training: analyzing customer requirements |
| 7 weeks after | | | Action skills training: identifying root causes |
| 8 weeks after | | Valuing differences | Action skills training: exploring alternatives |
| 9 weeks after | | | Action skills training: implementing improvements |
| 9 to 14 weeks after | | (Team leaders provide coaching and reinforcement) | (Team members actually implement their planned improvement) |
| 14 weeks after | | | Action skills training: evaluating the project |
| 16 weeks after | | • Performance planning and feedback training (followed by actually setting process and results objectives)<br>• Team development and diagnosis | |

| Time | | |
| --- | --- | --- |
| 4 months after | —Renewal Activity— | |
| 5 months after | Leadership team assesses its performance | (Team leaders prepare to deliver additional training) Gaining team agreement |
| 6 months after | | Assessing team performance |
| 1 year after | —Renewal Activity— | |
| 1 year to 18 months after | | Team members start to pursue their own needs and interests: making presentations, budgeting, etc. |
| 18 months after | —Refresher Training in Leadership Skills— | |
| 18 months to 2 years after | Team leaders support team members; prepare to deliver additional training | Refresher training in basic interaction skills, including handling conflict, influencing others, and supporting others |
| 2 years after | —Renewal Activity— | |

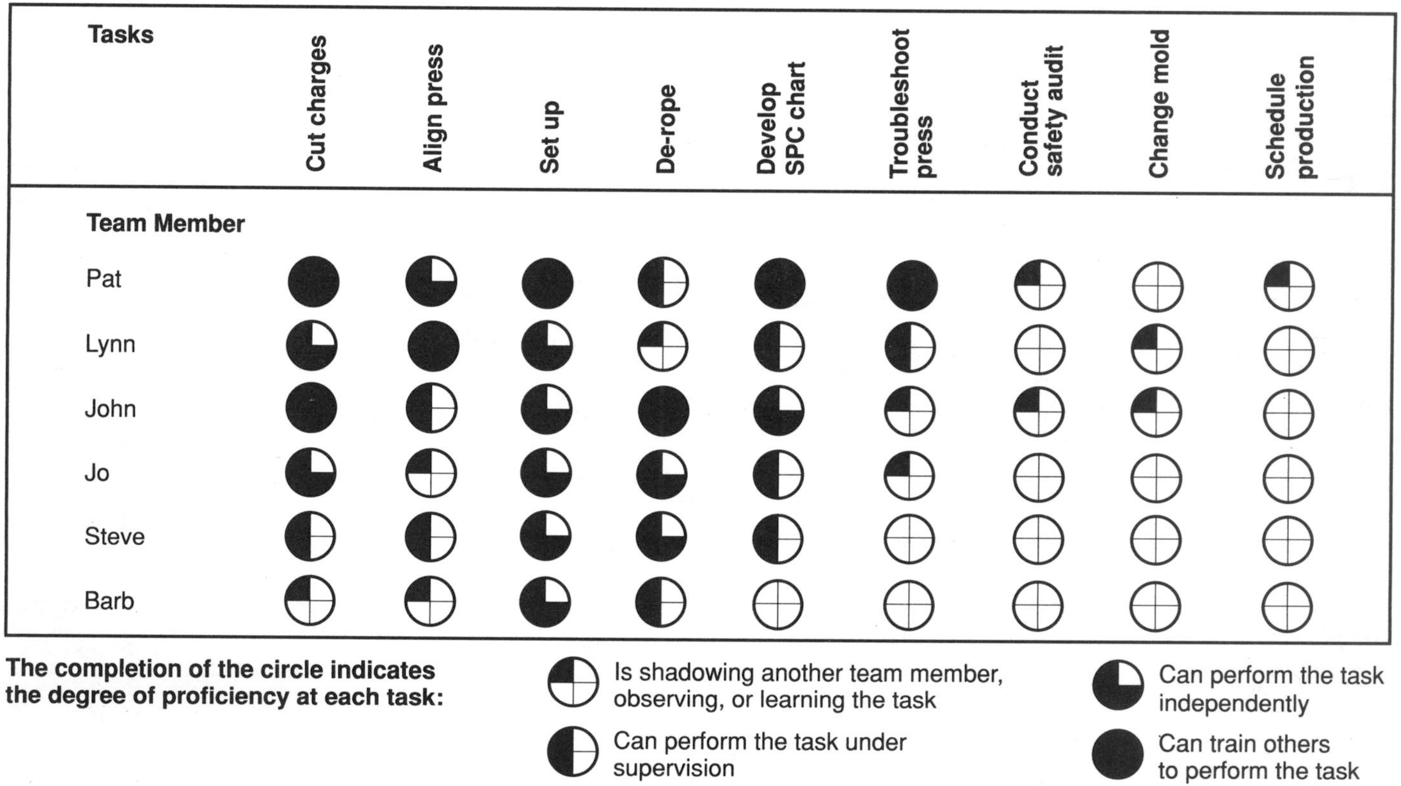

**Tasks**

| Team Member | Cut charges | Align press | Set up | De-rope | Develop SPC chart | Troubleshoot press | Conduct safety audit | Change mold | Schedule production |
|---|---|---|---|---|---|---|---|---|---|
| Pat | | | | | | | | | |
| Lynn | | | | | | | | | |
| John | | | | | | | | | |
| Jo | | | | | | | | | |
| Steve | | | | | | | | | |
| Barb | | | | | | | | | |

**The completion of the circle indicates the degree of proficiency at each task:**

◕ Is shadowing another team member, observing, or learning the task

◑ Can perform the task under supervision

◔ Can perform the task independently

● Can train others to perform the task

**Figure 9.2.** Team cross-training matrix.

operator would increase the temperature, the other would correct for it, causing the first to make even greater adjustments, and so on. This continued until management and the union instituted cross-training, and the two operators began to understand the larger process and the nature of their interdependency. Only then were they able to cooperate to maintain a steady, balanced state (Ketchum, 1984).

To facilitate cross-training, team members can take responsibility for their own training and development by setting up a skill matrix. A skill matrix lists all the skills required of a given team and monitors the degree of proficiency in each skill for each team member. One example is illustrated in Figure 9.2. As you walk through team-centered plants, you will often find such charts displayed prominently in the teams' areas. In this way team members can see at a glance where to find their team's experts and, therefore, the help they need. The charts also provide visual signals for leaders and team members alike to reinforce cross-training programs.

## TEAM TIPS

A lack of effective training is the number-one barrier to successful team implementation. Whether an organization offers enough training—and the right kind of training—can mean success or failure for its conversion. Following are a few lessons to consider as you put together team training plans.

### Support and Reinforce Training

Leadership support and reinforcement of training are critical. A work team facilitator once commented, ''We've spent a fortune training team members in skills their leaders won't let them use." Don't let this happen to you. Make specific provisions to train leaders so that they can coach, model, and reinforce the skills you want in your team members. Don't assume that this will come naturally to the leaders.

## Don't Allow Organizational Systems to Subvert Training

Your organizational structure, policies, and practices often inadvertently undermine the very behaviors you are trying to promote through training. We have all observed cases in which team members go through a mandatory sixteen hours of training in meeting management and come back to a job where there is no time or space to meet. A classic example of a system barrier was a situation in a large insurance company, where a team leader carefully analyzed the value-added activities in her team after completing training in quality/action skills. She determined that three separate processes were not contributing to customer requirements, so she transferred six people to an "upstream" team. She received a great deal of positive recognition for her efforts and felt proud of this accomplishment—until it came time for her annual review. At the review, her manager explained that she would not be receiving an increase this year, and probably not for the next three years, because the organization's compensation system paid according to how many people reported to each manager.

## Be Aware of the Stress of Continual Learning

Continual learning may be a strain for people and the system. Many team-centered plants establish a value for "continual learning" or "use of knowledge." This runs directly counter to our culture, which holds that learning is acquired early in life from accredited experts and that, when formal schooling ends, learning gives way to work. As a result, our capacity and ability to learn atrophies. Be prepared for some lack of tolerance for learning, especially in the early stages. Subaru-Isuzu solved this problem by creating a special course on "Learning to Learn" to help reorient team members toward a learning environment.

## Use Spaced Training

Spaced training works better than massed training. Whenever you are given a choice between providing training in massed segments or distributed ones, consider the training content. Training in most interpersonal skills works best if there is time between training sessions for individuals to practice their newly acquired skills. For example, at the team leader and group leader level, providing training four hours a week for ten weeks is more effective than providing forty hours of intensive training over a one-week period. In addition to the opportunity to apply skills, this schedule avoids the boredom and fatigue that accompany "going back to school."

When people have been away from classroom situations for years, it takes a while for team members to learn how to exercise "a whole new set of muscles," as one team coordinator at Hannaford Brothers Co. commented. He wasn't referring to the *brain* but to the *bottom*.

## Evaluate the Effectiveness of Training

Given what organizations invest in training, too little effort is made to evaluate training effectiveness. Although this evaluation is sometimes difficult to accomplish, the efficacy of a training program should be evaluated in terms of the application of skills on the job.

"Happiness" ratings obtained immediately after training are often misleading. If nothing else, participants in the training program should be surveyed a month or more afterward to see how the skills are being applied and whether any barriers exist that may prevent the participants from using these skills. Sophisticated methodologies, including the use of instruments and simulations to evaluate skills acquisition, are available and should be used if a significant commitment to training is being made at any level.

There are values from training that go far beyond merely improving team effectiveness:

- Team members and leaders gain an opportunity to grow in ways that they previously might never have thought possible and thus feel good about themselves.

- Many of the newly acquired skills can also be used outside the workplace in a wide variety of home and social situations. As interpersonal skills improve, relationships away from the workplace should show similar improvement.

- Management is sending a message that it is really serious about empowerment and constant improvement. The commitment of time and resources to training is far more impressive than any speech management might make.

# PART

## III

# BUILDING STRONG TEAMS

Organizations building empowered teams can lose sight of the fact that teams are both business entities and social groups. Like families, teams consist of a number of partners that live together five days a week for eight or more hours a day. Unlike families, teams are composed of members with diverse attitudes, values, and backgrounds. Because of this diversity, learning to work together requires time, patience, and effort.

As teams mature, they pass through four stages of development: (1) Getting Started, (2) Going in Circles, (3) Getting on Course, and (4) Full Speed Ahead. These stages have been called different things by different team experts, but the point being made is the same: Teams mature and evolve over time.

The goal of teams can be stated as follows:

Highly effective teams are composed of groups of committed individuals who trust each other; have a clear sense of purpose about their work; are effective communicators within and outside the team; make sure everyone in the team is involved in decisions affecting the group; and follow a process that helps them plan, make decisions, and ensure the quality of their work.

In Chapters Ten to Thirteen, these six key factors of team development—commitment, trust, purpose, communication, involvement, and process orientation— are compared as they relate to the four stages of team development. Paying attention to these factors might or might not make the journey to empowered work teams shorter, but it probably will make the ride smoother.

# KEY FACTORS IN TEAM DEVELOPMENT

## Commitment

Team members see themselves as belonging to a team rather than as individuals who operate autonomously. They are committed to group goals above and beyond their personal goals.

## Trust

Team members have faith in each other to honor their commitments, maintain confidences, support each other, and generally behave in a consistent and predictably acceptable fashion.

## Purpose

The team understands how it fits into the overall business of the organization. Team members know their roles, feel a sense of ownership, and can see how they make a difference.

## Communication

Communication refers to the style and extent of interactions both among members and between members and those outside the team. It also refers to the way that members handle conflict, decision making, and day-to-day interactions.

## Involvement

Everyone has a role in the team. Despite differences, team members must feel a sense of partnership with each other. Contributions are respected and solicited, and a real consensus is established before committing the team to action.

## Process Orientation

Once a team has a clear purpose (why it's together and where it's going), it must have a process or means to get there. The process should include problem-solving tools, planning techniques, regular meetings, meeting agendas and minutes, and accepted ways of dealing with problems.

CHAPTER

10

# STAGE ONE:
## Getting Started

I n the beginning, a team is
only a diverse collection of
individuals. Its members
are not clearly linked by goals
and roles. They are uncertain
about what to expect and are
not totally willing to commit
themselves to the process since
they are not yet able to grasp
its full scope.

One of the first steps in
building a team is to help team
members see themselves as
independent *and* interdepen-
dent, by both design and

necessity. Designing a holistic work process to suit a team is an effective first step to unifying the group.

In essence, a team that is just starting out is not really a team, even though everyone might call it one. A group might have many team-like supports, creating the feeling that all these supports are serving the team. Don't fool yourself.

Some team-like supports, like caps and jackets, are symbolic; others are concrete, like team-based compensation systems that reward group output. Although supports help the group think of itself as a team, the team does not really start to evolve until it engages in daily work experiences together such as job rotation, periodic meetings, and frequent training. Having a clear plan helps members get over the feelings of strangeness and anticipation they experience during their first few weeks as team members. If they have been carefully chosen and involved, their enthusiasm might be as high as their expectations. Yet experience shows that while the idea has been theoretically *sold* to them, they may not yet know what they have *bought*.

Typically, employees placed in team environments will have long histories of recognition and reward for past individual initiative. However, these new team members will have neither the experience to work in concert with their peers nor the job focus to propel them into collaboration. At first glance, they will tend to look like a bunch of cowhands—which is exactly how they will behave during this formative first stage.

## STAGE ONE: FACTOR INDICATORS

### Commitment

The team isn't really a team. Individuals are at the "Who am I?" stage. They question each other and withhold their full participation.

## Trust

Trust consists of "wait and see." There is as yet no basis to build upon.

## Purpose

In general, the purpose and mission of the team are understood but do not yet motivate.

## Communication

Communication is mostly tentative; it goes from leader to members and back again in the form of questions and explanations.

## Involvement

Involvement is mixed. More assertive members may hold center stage.

## Process Orientation

The process is new and unfamiliar. Individuals might be confused and are apt to rely on diverse individual experiences.

---

# TEAM EIGHT AT STAGE ONE

To get a sense of what a team is going through at this point, we return to Tom Marshall's team, which you met in our Prologue.

When Tom's team—Team Eight—formed five years ago, it had a particularly difficult time getting started. Because the teams at Tom's plant were formed as a result of the introduction of new technology, equipment problems exacerbated the interpersonal difficulties that would normally be expected when teams are launched. Team members became frustrated when they couldn't get everything to work properly. Barry, one of the team members, got so fed up with the lack of progress that he finally charged off to the engineering department. He came back more annoyed than ever, complaining that he had received a technical "lecture" from one of the process engineers. In the meantime, the rest of the team stood around the equipment arguing over the proper course of action.

Eventually the team turned to Karen, the newly appointed team leader, to help "fix" the problem. But Karen wasn't much help. Her desire to prove herself as an empowering team leader, and to produce results, only led to further confusion and stress.

Fortunately, the team's frustration with the situation showed up on the design team's "Three-Month Temperature Check" survey. With Team Eight's ratings mired at the bottom of the satisfaction scale, the plant's internal facilitator contacted the team to help it work through its problems. Through survey feedback, one-on-one coaching of the team leader, and facilitated meetings with the engineering support team, the facilitator was able to get Team Eight back on track. In fact, the session with Engineering resulted in a special team trip to the equipment vendor and additional training.

One other incident early in the team's development served to shore up its commitment to the process. Shortly after the conversion to teams, there was a ceremonial unlocking of the tool crib as a symbol of trust. Not long after that, several thousand dollars' worth of tools was discovered missing. The members of Team Eight held their collective breath and waited for management to replace the lock. Instead, the problem was turned over to the plant-wide safety and security team, and the crib remained unlocked. Everyone felt more secure in the organization's commitment to the team process.

# Helping Stage One Teams

There are many things organizations can do to nurture Stage One teams. Since the primary issue is helping them develop a sense of "teamness," one of the most helpful activities is to ask each team to write its own charter or mission statement. This single activity goes a long way toward clarifying the team's real purpose, allowing members to get to know each other while working on a non-conflict-laden task, and building commitment toward a larger unifying goal. This was such a positive experience for one of the teams at a General Electric Medical System's plant that the team had T-shirts printed with their newly developed mission statement on the back—and took great delight in explaining that mission to all the plant's visitors.

As with any kind of change, knowing what to expect is a big part of the coping process. In other words, the team should know what it's in for, so we strongly recommend that the design team publish and discuss the full implementation plan. It will be very reassuring to the teams to know that additional support and training will be provided and that they are not expected to become best buddies or high-performance teams overnight.

Team leaders should be prepared to acknowledge and empathize with the members' feelings of confusion, ambivalence, or even annoyance. Unfortunately, many leaders are tempted to dismiss them or even try to argue the members out of their feelings. And the last thing you want team members to "learn" this early in the game is that they have to suppress their concerns or find other outlets for them. Facilitators might want to warn the team that such early frustrations and letdowns are common. If the team members know what to expect, they might handle their feelings with awareness rather than resistance. During Stage One, teams should be encouraged to focus on "doable" projects rather than on internal processes. We have seen too many teams immediately tackle virtually insoluble group dynamics issues and, as a result, experience early failure. By first focusing on technical issues, the team can develop the confidence and internal insights needed to tackle the more difficult process issues at a later time.

## ADVANCING THROUGH STAGE ONE

Assuming that most things go right, the next problem likely to arise during the first few months in the life of a team is the letdown feeling, "So this is it?" At this point, team and design committee members are experiencing the settling-down effects that follow the high of a new job.

A certain amount of burnout is also to be expected when team members take on too many new responsibilities at once. The strain might result from working in a team, learning new tasks, working in a new part of the operation or in a new position, adjusting to new work rules or the absence of new rules, and dealing with people and issues that are quite different from the ones encountered previously.

Team members in Stage One also thirst for clear definitions and boundaries. They need to work with the organization's leaders and facilitators to define work expectations and the boundaries of their authority and responsibility. Keep in mind that unlike other types of teams, self-directed teams must cope with new ways of approaching both the *doing* and *managing* aspects of work.

To move through this first stage, teams spend a large amount of time in training. Many organizations make the mistake of allowing training to wait until a team forms, letting it find its way by trial and error. This can interfere with individual and team development. Organizations that place a high value on training their teams have learned a valuable lesson: An early investment in helping individuals learn their jobs puts to rest many of the fears associated with the question: "Can I do it?"

Basic interpersonal skills that will help the group coalesce include:

- Communicating one-on-one
- Coping with interpersonal conflict
- Participating in group problem-solving or planning meetings
- Listening, questioning, and providing feedback

It is also helpful for the team to make plant visits, learning what other teams are doing, finding out what problems these teams faced, and seeing how they handled them. This provides the team with positive models and a chance to ask questions that members may secretly harbor about what can happen to the team over time.

11

# STAGE TWO:
## Going in Circles

As the natural assimilation process continues, questions like "Who am I and who are you?" turn into "What do we do and how do we do it?" Individuals begin to feel more comfortable as they develop a better sense of what a team is and how they are expected to work together in that team. While Stage One, Getting Started, often can be confusing and stressful, it is marked by the excitement of being *new*. In Stage Two the honeymoon is over. As one team member put it, "Work is still work. We still have to get up and come here in the morning."

People also begin to face up to the fact that they are being asked to handle aspects of work that are new to most of them. The team becomes involved with work planning, problem solving, team meetings, and other new duties, besides maintaining responsibilities for their jobs. They may feel time pressure and confusion; for instance, they might struggle with deciding who will handle these new tasks.

Out of this confusion arises stress about roles in the team and about members' usefulness. This type of questioning tests the cohesiveness of the team. Instead of uniting behind a common goal, the team tends to pull apart, sampling different ways to meet the problems it faces.

A typical stress reaction with novice team members is the urge to pull out of the team and work alone. This is a legitimate response, and one that some feel will cut through the time-consuming effort of getting others to understand and agree with the work process.

Team leaders, group leaders, and managers experience their own problems at this stage. They continue to grapple with how much responsibility and control to relinquish. If the team is floundering, there is a natural reaction to step in and take over. As one senior manager in an automotive plastics company that was starting a high-involvement plant said, "The worst thing you can do is call me in to visit if things aren't going right. I may not be able to keep myself from telling everyone what to do differently."

Going in Circles is a perfectly natural evolutionary stage and one that is important for the development of the group. Much like a maturing teenager seeking autonomy, the team has to experience conflict and rejection before it can enjoy success. If it doesn't learn to handle stress early, it certainly won't be able to handle it later on.

This is the stage during which even the most motivated teams experience the greatest letdown. They have been on the job for several months, have received significant amounts of training, and are now encountering new job challenges daily. They are settling into a routine, demands are increasing, and the energy of their fast start is dissipating. Teams embarking on Stage Two are between worlds. They do not yet provide to each other social and emotional support, yet new organizational expectations demand that they function as a highly cohesive unit.

## STAGE TWO: FACTOR INDICATORS

### Commitment

Commitment tends to be toward subgroups, not toward the team as a whole.

### Trust

Members sort out those they trust, those they don't trust, and those who are still unknown.

### Purpose

The team is developing a greater sense of purpose but needs reassurance and guidance.

### Communication

As members assert themselves, conflicts arise. Communication may be direct and aggressive.

### Involvement

Some members still dominate the group.

### Process Orientation

"Standard" processes are just beginning to emerge, but are still unfamiliar and difficult for the team to use.

---

# TEAM EIGHT IN STAGE TWO

Six months after start-up, Team Eight finally stabilized its production process, but it seemed to Karen that the team had started to splinter into two factions. Barry, Leon, and Mike quickly mastered the technical aspects of the work. All three progressed rapidly through the cross-training matrix and were now responsible for training others in job skills. Tom, Linda, Karen, and Joe were lagging behind in job skills training, largely because they had volunteered for plant-wide committees and other special assignments. Barry, Leon, and Mike complained that they had to "carry" the team, and the others resented this perceived elitist attitude.

At about this time, Joe adjusted a press incorrectly, which resulted in six hours of downtime and the scrapping of $22,000 worth of product. The plant manager asked to see Joe the next day, and Joe—who came from a company with a rather autocratic culture—was certain that he was about to be fired. Instead, the plant manager, borrowing a humorous line from IBM founder Tom Watson, said, "Why should I fire you now? I just invested $22,000 in your education." Joe was greatly relieved, and he confided that much of his problem was caused by tension in the team and by his fear of approaching other team members with questions. Together Joe, Karen, and the plant manager raised the issue of team communication at the next team meeting and gained the team's commitment to pay special attention to this area.

The facilitator, who met with the team for several sessions, noticed that the meetings were unproductive and tended to be another source of frustration for some members. The facilitator helped the team work out the following standard agenda to keep them focused:

1. Review plant and team mission statement.

2. Discuss team performance compared to goals.

3. Discuss what has been learned.

4. Decide what action should be taken.

5. Plan how to operate more effectively as a team.

The agenda proved to be so effective that eventually it was adopted by other teams. In spite of this progress, however, the team still experienced turnover. Barry left the team for a lower-paying job at another company. The team became concerned about being the first to lose a member, especially because Barry had been so vocal about "the stupid team concept" on his way out. Throughout, Karen kept the team positively focused on the task of selecting a new member. Team members enjoyed learning interviewing skills and being empowered to make their own selection decision.

## HELPING STAGE TWO TEAMS

This is perhaps the most critical point in your team's development process. Conflict and dissatisfaction can be extremely disconcerting to those who want the team to succeed, and these emotions bring all the critics out of the closet ready to say, "I told you so."

You can head this off at the pass by continuing to practice the no-surprises school of team design. The more information you give people about what to expect, the better prepared and less anxious they will be. In that spirit, many organizations actually run "preparation sessions" four to eight months after their conversion to teams. In these sessions, facilitators explain that feelings of increasing tension are a normal part of the team development process and that the increased pressure a team may feel actually can be used to help it forge a closer bond. In some cases, organizations ask a mature team to conduct a panel discussion describing its own experience and reassuring everyone that there is life after Stage Two.

If the design team effectively monitors team attitudes and development, it should be able to predict when "preparation sessions" will be needed. Another way to counteract growing feelings of dissatisfaction is to sponsor celebrations of team achievements. Recognizing and publicizing even the smallest accomplishments help to maintain a sense of hope for team members.

## ADVANCING THROUGH STAGE TWO

This is the "What do we do?" stage. To make the best of the interpersonal skills acquired during Stage One training, team members need to develop norms that are reinforced by clear roles and expectations.

Because job responsibilities are still being sorted out and management may be struggling for direction, the group may squabble about *who* should do *what*. To facilitate smooth progress during this stage, the focus should shift to ways of organizing the work and deploying resources to get various jobs done.

Collectively, the team should become more accomplished in the following skills:

- Leading and participating in meetings
- Supporting others in doing their jobs

- Exercising influence to get information and support
- Valuing diversity
- Presenting ideas
- Gathering and organizing information

The greater the focus on process, the more energy the team can devote to building relationships. At this stage it is essential to "trust the process." Have faith that by following the problem-solving techniques, using the training models in interactions, and taking the time to respect and listen to one another, positive results will follow. Above all, patience is the key to evolving into the next stage.

CHAPTER

12

# Stage Three:
## Getting on Course

As the team adjusts and its members become comfortable with one another, everyone begins to concentrate on the job at hand. The team increasingly becomes more goal focused and develops routines for handling crises, new situations, and problems. Team members begin to sort out their responsibilities and rely on each other's talents. Not everyone performs all jobs at the same level; rather, some informal ''experts'' emerge, such as those who can lead team meetings, present ideas effectively, talk to Engineering or Maintenance and get results, or put things in writing—and a few will prove to be most effective when they are left to work independently.

In this stage, team members accept diversity, personal style, and the need for different skills and talents in getting the *entire* job done. This implies trust, which is brought about by experiencing both smoothly running and stressful situations and by recognizing that without individual differences, there can be little collective creativity.

At the same time that the team is learning to capitalize on differences, each team member is becoming a master at every team job. Cross-training is taking hold, enabling team members to rely on one another to fill in or handle peaks in production and service demands. A well-executed cross-training plan helps create the feeling that "We're all in this together."

One potential problem at this stage is that team members may swear allegiance to the team above the organization. This can manifest itself in the form of elitism or protection of the team from others in the organization. One problem with elitism is that team members may be unwilling to confront problems and issues with others in their team for fear of rocking the boat. Fortunately, leaders in this stage are usually more comfortable with the concept of empowerment and self-direction. On the whole, they are beginning to trust and understand the team process better. As things begin to gel, team leaders are more likely to relinquish control and become comfortable with their roles as "coaches."

## STAGE THREE: FACTOR INDICATORS

### Commitment

Team members are committed to getting the job done.

### Trust

Members are developing trust based on the experience of working together.

### Purpose

The focus is on performance and achieving team goals.

### Communication

Primarily, task-oriented communication exists within the team. Team members begin to develop relationships with support groups outside the team.

### Involvement

Most members are comfortable with their roles in the team.

### Process Orientation

Team processes become more fluid and, thus, more natural.

---

# TEAM EIGHT AT STAGE THREE

Slightly more than a year into the team process, things began to run smoothly for Team Eight. They were taking on more responsibility and becoming involved in working with two key suppliers on a quality improvement process. They improved their team productivity and came up with unique ways to reduce cycle time.

They did encounter a problem with one team member who seemed to be volunteering for more interteam assignments than time allowed for, affecting the performance levels of the full team. The team complained to the group leader and facilitator who, rather than taking over, encouraged the team to give feedback to the team member directly. They did, and the team member immediately corrected the problem. Until he was approached, he had been unaware of the effect he was having on the team.

The facilitator was pleased to note a great deal of pride within the team. The plant and the team recently had been featured in an article on empowered organizations in a national publication, and spirits were high. The facilitator capitalized on the team's desire to live up to its newly won external reputation, and on its heightened task orientation. This was done by involving the team in organizing and handling the many requests for plant tours it was receiving. This had a number of positive effects on team members: (1) it turned their task orientation outward and gave them a broader appreciation for the plant's functioning as a whole, (2) it helped them understand other departments' needs and functions at a time when interteam conflicts were likely to erupt, and (3) it provided an opportunity to further develop the team's communication skills.

At the same time, the original design team experienced difficulty in getting anyone to reevaluate the original design. Although continuous improvement was one of the plant's values, everyone seemed more interested in protecting the original structure than in improving it. This caused problems with the plant's plans to add two new product lines. The design team decided to schedule a "renewal workshop" to reinforce the original values and generate commitment to a redesign effort. The workshop was successful and ultimately resulted in changing the roles of a half-dozen leaders to external support specialists, who were responsible for special engineering and training assignments.

## HELPING TEAMS IN STAGE THREE

The biggest challenge to organizations with teams in this stage is to broaden their focus: to expand beyond their natural internal orientation. Fortunately, there are several things your organization can do to turn your teams' attention inside out:

- Conduct most of the training at this stage in interdisciplinary groups. Although early training often is conducted in intact work groups, in later stages teams will benefit more from interacting with other teams and support groups.

- Encourage more contact with customers and suppliers. Customer requirements become a superordinate goal that can stimulate cooperation between teams. We have witnessed remarkable transformations in cases where several teams have been sent to consult with an external customer about a particular problem. Suddenly they understand the impact of maximizing their own team's performance at the expense of another's.

- Work with other levels of the organization. The more often team members can "helicopter up" and resolve problems from a broader business perspective, the less competitive teams become.

## ADVANCING THROUGH STAGE THREE

The predominant characteristic of the team at this stage is its cohesiveness and internal orientation. Moving on requires broader goal orientation. Team members need to get involved in larger organizational issues and receive enhanced training in overall business goals in order to make more informed decisions.

Since the team is fully capable of organizing and improving its own work methods and processes, it benefits most from advanced problem-solving techniques that can systematically help it move beyond "the low-hanging fruit"—the obvious improvement opportunities. In addition, teams can take advantage of training to expand their job depth. For example, they can accept more of the maintenance responsibilities that traditionally were reserved for "specialists" outside the team.

Also, continued focus on training in interpersonal and communication skills cannot be ignored. Skills in advanced feedback and listening are critical if team members are to be responsible for helping other members through the rough spots of dealing with internal and external suppliers and customers.

It is at this stage that innovative, shared compensation systems can be most effective. The group is now capable of putting forward a united effort and must be motivated to do so. Gain sharing and other types of team bonuses now can be given serious consideration. Incentives before this stage might not have had nearly as profound an effect on production as they will now.

# STAGE FOUR:
## Full Speed Ahead

I t takes years of working together to achieve this high-end, advanced level of team functioning. In this stage, teams constantly strive to be proactive by anticipating demands, demonstrating the need for additional resources, identifying training, improving their critical indicators, and moving into new areas of responsibility.

Teams in Stage Four are focused on much more than continuous improvement of operations. Teams begin to develop expectations about their "rights" and insist on the freedom to exercise those rights, which include being consulted on decisions affecting the team, being listened to, sharing in the growth and profitability of the enterprise to which the team belongs, and having input into the direction the organization is taking. A proactive team is, in the truest sense, *a team*. When a team is not allowed to grow proactively, it will slip precipitously back into earlier stages.

Fully self-directed teams challenge the sacred cow of the power of the leadership position. Teams at this level want to hire their own members, ask for business information that might previously have been considered confidential, and seek a piece of the action based on their contribution to profitability. They will not tolerate autocratic supervision and management. In essence, they demand a democratic workplace.

One food products company was faced with a team revolt of sorts when management decided to replace two group leaders who were being transferred to another location. The teams felt that the positions were no longer needed.

In most cases, Stage Four leaders are truly comfortable with the concept and benefits of empowerment. Managers and leaders finally realize that their jobs *do* have value. We heard a story from a manager who helped lead the charge toward self-direction in her own service organization. Five years earlier, she was a line employee in the same department; when she was transferred out of the department, she swore that she would never come back, especially as a manager. However, she did return and now loves her job.

## STAGE FOUR: FACTOR INDICATORS

### Commitment

The team is committed both to the organization and to itself.

## Trust

Trust is extended openly. It is a more stable commodity than mistrust. For new members, failure is engineered out of the system.

## Purpose

A clear vision and sense of mission are maintained. The team is also flexible and able to adapt to changing business demands.

## Communication

Communication is complex. It is self-initiated on an as-needed basis. Frequent team meetings, once an invariant fact of life, may even be sacrificed to the changing communication needs of this group.

## Involvement

Involvement is constant within the team. Even reticent members become involved, making presentations and taking leadership roles. Teams might be involved in product and process innovations.

## Process Orientation

Team processes are a regular part of work and are no longer seen as add-ons; in fact, they are second nature. Continuous improvement and quality become internal values.

---

# TEAM EIGHT AT STAGE FOUR

Two years into the process, after more advancing than backsliding and with the addition of two new team members, Team Eight is going full speed ahead. Several team members have asked for additional responsibility in preparing not only the team's budget but the plant's budget as well. Tom and Leon are on a plant-wide task force to consider a capacity expansion, and the team as a whole has taken on the responsibility of developing its own forecasts for labor efficiency and scrap reduction.

Because similar growth is taking place in other teams, the production manager finds himself without enough to do. When he asks for a transfer, headquarters puts him in charge of a new team-oriented start-up.

Three years into the process, the plant is doing very well as a result of teams:

- It is the number-one quality supplier in its business group.

- It has 20 percent fewer leaders and support staff than at the beginning.

- It is a model for four other plants that have begun their journey toward empowered teams.

## Remaining in Stage Four

The work team that is truly self-directed and that functions as a cohesive team and business unit constitutes an accomplishment to be savored and a goal to keep any team busy for quite some time. Staying at this level, however, sometimes involves even more work than it takes to move through the earlier stages. Teams at Stage Four are involved not only in work process improvement but also in improvements that go beyond the factory floor. They may play an active role in organizing a plant's total quality improvement plan by introducing new technology, developing improved vendor and customer relationships, or changing product specifications.

To be effective in these new roles, the team needs to learn more about the business. Training can focus on business skills, learning how to interpret business reports, and using diagnostics such as inventory turns, cost of quality, return on investment or equity, depreciation schedules, cost calculations, reduction of cycle times, and other measures of manufacturing effectiveness.

In addition, a team might take a more active role in its self-management by identifying criteria for selection, conducting interviews, making hiring decisions, or administering other personnel processes (such as performance appraisal or discipline) within the team. To do this, team members need training in selecting, appraising, and managing performance. They might also be held responsible for allocating rewards among team members based on performance.

One of the most effective ways to keep a team at this advanced level of functioning is to give it responsibility for mentoring other less advanced teams. It forces the Stage Four team to think about what has contributed to its success and helps it recognize any symptoms of slippage. It also reinforces the team's identity as a successful group, which in turn motivates the team to maintain that status.

## TEAM TIPS

Teams progress at varying rates, depending on both internal and external influences. As your teams advance through the four stages and utilize the six key factors, they should keep the following tips in mind.

## Consider Those Outside the Team

Whatever model you adopt, don't forget that team development is not solely an internal phenomenon that only the team goes through. The team develops in conjunction with environmental influences that include management practices, facilities, technologies, and the structures and systems that form the policies and work practices of the organization.

As the team develops into a semiautonomous unit, it rubs up against its natural support structure. Engineering, administration, sales, field service, design, and planning are a few of the internal areas that deal directly with team members. This is often a new experience for support people who are accustomed to meeting only with supervisors and managers.

Adjustments must take place on both sides. Managers must learn to feel comfortable making commitments to employees and should ensure quality team decisions by coaching rather than by checking with management. Similarly, employees must become comfortable speaking up in meetings; making presentations; using data, charts, and graphs; and leading meetings. They must develop good interactive skills in order to deal with the types of problems that occur when priorities conflict or approaches vary. They no longer can become frustrated and argue without facts. Nor can they become discouraged and chalk it up to management.

In short, team members have to learn to operate more like managers, and managers and professional support staff must operate as part of a larger team. The process is a learning experience for both groups.

## Don't Expect a Linear Process

Team development is not necessarily a linear process. Many teams and facilitators make the mistake of assuming that once a team achieves a certain level of functioning, it can only get better. Unfortunately, changes in team functioning do not always occur in a positive direction. We have observed teams slip for various reasons:

- *New members.* The addition of new members often causes teams to revisit Stages One and Two briefly as the new members struggle with purpose, commitment, and trust.

- *Team trauma.* A significant emotional event in the life of a team might cause the team to catapult into a more advanced or regressed state. In one case, a significant loss of market share for one team's product resulted in more frequent conflicts and caused the team to slip back into Stage Two functioning.

- *Crises of faith.* Management behavior can seriously undermine the team's sense of purpose, commitment, and trust.

- *Lack of attention or maintenance.* Without training and development, team functioning and cohesiveness can gradually erode.

## Accommodate Different Rates of Progress

You can't expect to force everyone through a lockstep process of development. As with any developmental process, you should be prepared to accommodate those who are ready for greater responsibility as well as those who are having difficulty keeping up with the team's progress. This is where many organizations have found internal consultants to be especially helpful. Facilitators can match aggressive team members with external challenges and responsibilities and provide one-on-one coaching for those who lag behind.

## Monitor Individual and Team Progress

It is critical to establish some measure of individual and team development. We recommend both intra- and interteam measures. Team level assessments are best administered and processed by the teams themselves. Aggregate measures are necessary only on a quarterly basis to help the organization plan group training, development, and renewal activities.

We have developed an instrument that assesses team performance on each of the six team empowerment factors discussed throughout this chapter. A sample of some of the items for the "Commitment" factor are contained in Figure 13.1. Assessment is important, but so is what the team does with the data. Remember that information from any assessment tool should be used as a guide for action and training to help the team progress more rapidly.

# RESEARCH STUDY ON TEAMS' STAGES OF DEVELOPMENT

We recently conducted a research study using the instrument partially shown in Figure 13.1. The purpose of the study was to get a better feel for where teams are in terms of the stages of development. The organizations that participated, both manufacturing and service, have been operating with teams anywhere from six months to three years. More than 120 leaders responded to the survey. These leaders were either group leaders or managers "outside" the actual teams.

Two leaders rated each team on its overall stage of team development (Getting Started, Going in Circles, Getting on Course, and Full Speed Ahead) as well as on each of the individual factors. For the overall stage on team development, the leaders reported that 6 percent of the teams were in Stage One, 30 percent in Stage Two, 47 percent in Stage Three, and 14 percent in Stage Four. Seventy-eight percent of the leaders reported that they were either generally or highly confident in their performance ratings.

## Team Factor Survey

**Rating Scale**
1 = Does Not Apply
2 = Rarely (About 20% of the time)
3 = Sometimes (About 40% of the time)
4 = Frequently (About 70% of the time)
5 = Almost Always (About 90% of the time)

**Team members:**

1. Stay late, come to work early, or take work home to make sure a job gets done.

2. Attend regularly scheduled team meetings.

3. Successfully complete work assignments that were set by the team.

4. Try to improve the quality of work performed by the team.

5. Talk about their concerns with the quality of the work done by the team.

6. Speak favorably about the team to others.

7. Help each other when necessary.

8. Go outside the team for help or resources when the team can't solve a problem by itself.

9. Live up to their responsibilities.

**Figure 13.1.** Sample measuring items for the team factor "Commitment."

10. Get to meetings on time.

11. Spend their free time (such as lunch, breaks, and after-work hours) with other team members.

12. Work hard to fulfill the responsibilities assigned to them by the team.

13. Try to find solutions when there are problems with the team's level of performance.

14. Remain positive when things don't go well for the team.

15. Talk enthusiastically about working together to achieve the team's goals.

16. Try hard not to let the team down.

17. Take on extra work when necessary to ensure that the team meets or exceeds its goals.

18. Want the team to be successful.

19. Are satisfied with the roles they have in the team.

20. Work to maintain a high level of team spirit and morale.

21. Take feedback about the team's performance seriously.

22. Think of themselves more as members of the team than as individuals.

**Figure 13.1**—*Continued*

# EPILOGUE

# WHAT'S NEXT FOR SELF-DIRECTED TEAMS?

I n this last section, we take a look at the growth of self-directed teams in the workplace, further expansion of the team concept into white-collar applications, and growing team involvement in higher levels of business decision making. We note international implications and call for more national support of this country's employee involvement activities. We comment on some union sensitivities, predict a team backlash, and conclude by providing an assessment of the future of the work team concept.

## THE SHIFT TOWARD TEAMS

In his book *Powershift*, Alvin Toffler discusses radical changes taking place in today's workplace (Toffler, 1990). He writes: "The old smokestack division of a firm into 'heads' and 'hands' no longer works. The knowledge load and, more important, the decision load, are being redistributed. In a continual circle of learning and unlearning and relearning, workers need to master new technologies, adapt to new organizational forms, and generate new ideas."

There is firm agreement from the shop floor to the boardroom: To compete effectively in today's workplace, work forces must continue to be empowered and decision making must be learned. Employee involvement is moving from the stage of curious experimentation to one of business necessity. Teams provide one of the most powerful and proven empowerment strategies—and, as such, their future is bright. But don't take our word for it!

Jerry Junkins, Texas Instrument's CEO, recently stated in *Fortune* magazine, "No matter what your business, those teams are the wave of the future" (Dumaine, 1990, p. 52). In the same article, Corning CEO Jamie Houghton said, "If you really believe in quality, when you cut through everything, it's empowering your people, and it's empowering your people that leads to teams" (p. 52).

Robert Hass, Levi Strauss's CEO, claimed, "I see us moving toward a team-oriented, multiskilled environment in which the team takes on many of the supervisor's and trainer's tasks. If you combine that with some sort of gain sharing, you probably will have a much more productive plant with higher employee satisfaction and commitment" (Howard, 1990). A recent cover story in *Time* singled out the General Motors Saturn's team approach as a strategy that will help keep the United States competitive in the global economy (Gwynne, 1990).

## EXPECT RAPID GROWTH

A report entitled *America's Choice: High Skills or Low Wages,* prepared by the National Center of Education and the Economy (1990), estimated that no more than 5 percent of U.S. companies have experimented seriously with high-involvement organizations. As we mentioned earlier, Edward Lawler further asserts that less than 2 percent of America's work force is organized into teams. If, as we maintain, empowerment is the key to the future of many organizations, and if organizations are just beginning to use teams, then we can expect rapid growth of the empowered team concept in the years ahead.

The Survey data support these expectations. The great majority of executives who responded to the Survey indicated that fewer than 10 percent of their work areas are currently organized into teams. These same executives anticipate that over 50 percent of their work forces will be organized into teams within five years. Similarly, 83 percent of the work team members, leaders, and practitioners who responded to the Survey expect to see self-directed teams expand in their organizations rapidly over the next three years.

## WHITE-COLLAR APPLICATIONS

The manufacturing sector of the economy has made the greatest strides in increasing productivity and quality by focusing on processes, technologies, and people. For the most part, teams were pioneered in the factory; subsequently, the great majority of team implementations have occurred in manufacturing settings.

However, white-collar and service industries are facing the same competitive pressures as those faced by manufacturing. They too are being required to reduce management layers, focus on quality, and drastically improve productivity to stay competitive. Thus, they are turning to employee involvement and empowerment, and many team efforts are already under way. Shenandoah Life Insurance Company, American Transtech, Aid Association for Lutherans (AAL), AT&T Operator Services, the St. Paul Companies, IDS Financial Services, and American Express Company all have successfully used the team concept. Let's take a closer look.

We have already shared the AAL story—perhaps the most widely publicized white-collar team application. AAL teams have advanced to assuming responsibility for their members' compensation. Each team is responsible for sharing in the management of its payroll budget and for certifying team members in AAL's pay-for-service system. AAL offers 167 possible services, and each member's base salary is determined by his or her primary service. The team is involved in certifying its members in additional skills if they need the service and have the budgetary funds available.

American Transtech, based in Jacksonville, Florida, provides another example of the application of teams in the service sector. Formerly AT&T's stock and bond division, American Transtech was spun off into an independent subsidiary, providing financial and marketing services. Historically, Transtech operated on a white-collar version of the industrial model, with a document traveling down an administrative line and each person adding something to the "product" along the way.

With its new team design, all major lease-processing functions are represented on each team. Therefore, one team can take responsibility for the business transaction from beginning to end. This enables teams to process 800 lease applications a day, compared with 400 a day under the previous structure.

Ravenswood Aluminum, a privately owned company with over $600 million in sales, transformed its inside customer service department into self-directed teams; the company is now exploring the use of this same concept with its outside sales staff.

The town government of Windsor, Connecticut, organized its small group of social work counselors into an empowered team. The members meet regularly, assign and schedule their own case loads, and handle their own hiring.

Both Corning and Texas Instruments have designed and implemented empowered teams in their white-collar support departments, such as Management Information Systems and Accounting, to serve their internal customers.

The concept of white-collar teams presents special challenges because it has always been difficult to measure the productivity of service organizations and because some white-collar work might make cross-training impossible or highly inefficient. For example, it would not be feasible to cross-train *everyone* to be lawyers, accountants, or marketing specialists. Nevertheless, while white-collar teams might take on a different appearance and set of challenges than those of manufacturing teams, their growth is imminent.

## "SELF-DIRECTED" ORGANIZATIONS

Although in the majority of cases "bosses" still "run the company," self-directed teams are assuming increasing responsibility for key business decisions. In several companies, we have seen empowerment expand outside the work team to involvement in decisions that affect businesses as a whole.

For example, Semco, the innovative Brazilian company referred to earlier, needed a larger plant in its marine division to produce pumps, compressors, and ship propellers. Initially the company farmed out the job of finding a location to several real estate agents, but to no avail. Semco then turned to its employees. Within a week employees located three prospective sites, all within a reasonable distance. Often participation stops with mere input, but Semco arranged for all its employees to inspect the three sites and then vote on which would be most appropriate for the plant's location. Although the employees selected a site that management did not really want, Semco purchased it anyway. In addition, the workers designed the layout, installed a flexible manufacturing system, and hired a prominent Brazilian artist to paint the new plant. The result: The division's productivity more than doubled, from $14,200 to $37,500 per employee (Semler, 1989).

At the new $3.5 billion GM Saturn plant in Tennessee, the labor agreement calls for consensus on decisions that affect team members in any way. So team members became involved in selecting the company's advertising agency and in choosing the suppliers of some electronic components. Saturn's United Auto Worker coordinator stated in *Time* magazine that to his knowledge, no other UAW workers have ever decided on the actual purchase and installation of equipment (Gwynne, 1990).

As the team concept takes hold and management begins trusting and believing in the value of empowerment, we expect team involvement to increase in decisions that affect the well-being of the entire business entity, not just the team.

## TEAMS INTERNATIONAL

Unfortunately, few data are available on how international applications of the team concept are faring—but we know that teams are growing. New opportunities are appearing on every continent; even the emerging Eastern European countries are experimenting with teams. Some of these teams in international settings are highly empowered; others less so. Volvo Corporation in Sweden, with one of the first team experiences, continues to build on that reputation and has progressively moved its teams along the empowerment scale. Berkel in Germany and Ebthoner A.G. in Switzerland are other examples of overseas applications. Other examples include NCR Corporation in Scotland and Intel Corporation in Singapore.

We often hear it said that teams started in Japan. Although it is true that the Japanese have been strong team players, it is unusual to see true self-directed teams in Japanese companies.

Certainly the concept of self-direction, to some extent, must be culturally bound. Highly autocratic or traditional work cultures and societies will hinder the move toward empowerment and teams. Yet, given our current highly competitive global economy coupled with dramatically changing workforce values worldwide, we predict that self-directed teams will become a unique and highly effective strategy that will continue to be exported worldwide.

# THE NEED FOR NATIONAL SUPPORT

Teams and other employee involvement activities may have spread more rapidly in countries such as Sweden and Japan as a result of national support. In Japan, for instance, the Japanese Union of Scientists and Engineers not only endorses quality circles philosophically but helps to install them in private companies. Sweden also actively supports employee involvement. For example, the Swedish Employer's Federation has served as a consultant to companies that express an interest in increasing participation.

Although there are isolated cases of state support for employee involvement, America lacks a powerful centralized impetus to increase participation in the workplace. One government initia-

tive that *has* worked is the Malcolm Baldrige National Quality
Award, which U.S. companies have pursued like the Holy Grail
since the award's establishment by Congress in 1987. For winners,
losers, and even spectators, the Baldrige has become a widely
accepted standard for running a good company. The award has
sparked interest not only in quality but also in the realization that
quality and empowerment are closely related. Many of the Baldrige winners (such as Milliken & Co., Xerox Corporation, and
IBM Corporation) have implemented empowered teams as part
of their total quality effort.

The recently published report *America's Choice: High Skills or
Low Wages* (National Center of Education and the Economy, 1990)
calls for national support to give employers more incentive to invest
in both the education of their workers and the pursuit of higher-
involvement work organizations. This report suggests expanded
awards for "best practice" organizations and the establishment
of a National Clearinghouse for the Reorganization of Work and
Work Force Skills Development. The report was issued with the
support of senior corporate leaders such as John Sculley of Apple
Computer, Jamie Houghton of Corning, and Kay Whitmore of
Eastman Kodak.

## THE ROLE OF ORGANIZED LABOR

In Chapter Three we reviewed several successful team implementations in union environments. On the whole, the leaderships of
various national unions—including the United Auto Workers, the
United Steelworkers of America, and the Communications Workers of America—have supported various forms of teams across the
United States.

The major form of union dissension comes from "splinter
groups" or from local unions. For example, a few years ago, the

UAW actually formed a group, ironically called "New Directions," that opposed the team concept. Mike Parker and Jane Slaughter published a collection of articles in a book called *Choosing Sides: Unions and the Team Concept* (1988) that reflects the views of this group and represents a strong union position against teams. Chapter titles include "Management by Stress," "Early Disenchantment," and "Teams Divide the Union." To date, however, New Directions has not received the support it had hoped to obtain.

Questions have also risen as to whether teams are permissible under the National Labor Relations Act, which bars employers from providing "financial or other support" to labor organizations. Under the Act, labor organizations are defined vaguely as "any organization of any kind, or any agency or employee representation committee or plan" that deals not only with wages and schedules, but also with "conditions of work."

In 1990, the Chemical Workers Association won a case against Du Pont's Chamber Works in Deepwater, New Jersey. Du Pont had established a design team that included twelve supervisors and eleven rank-and-file employees, but the union charged the team with violation of the federal labor law because it was an employer-dominated labor organization, even though the union president conceded that some of its membership was in favor of teams. As a result, Du Pont had to disband the team.

Despite such instances, we believe that the outlook for union involvement is positive. In Chapter Three, we noted that 53 percent of the organizations responding to the Survey had unions, yet only 6 percent of that group indicated that their unions opposed self-directed teams. Twenty-one percent indicated that their unions had adopted a neutral position toward teams. The remainder of the respondents—73 percent—showed a favorable disposition toward union involvement. Interestingly, executives who responded to the Survey indicated that lack of management support (32 percent) was a bigger problem than lack of union support (24 percent).

Many organizations have encouraged constructive roles for the union in their team implementations. At General Motors, for instance, the union role is established at each location, where the most critical factor seems to be the committee member's role. In most cases, team members can use the services of the committee member when needed. Union officials act as facilitators for team meetings or problem-solving sessions, thus performing much the same function as the team advisor (Cherry, 1982).

At New United Motors Manufacturing, the joint Toyota–General Motors operation in Fremont, California, key support members are paired with union representatives, attending meetings for each other, answering each other's phones, and so on. At Saturn, the union coordinator and the president share the same office space, often travel to meetings together, and collaborate on almost all key decisions. Finally, Corning's Blacksburg, Virginia, automatic filter plant has been so successful with teams that the American Flint Glass Workers Union is cooperating with a conversion to teams in several other Corning facilities.

The union, like management, must deal not only with external competitive pressures but also with the changing values of today's work force—values that include greater participation, autonomy, and flexibility. Teams that are developed and implemented collaboratively provide "wins" for both management and labor. As Lawrence Bankowski, a national union president, recently said, "Deep down manufacturers have to change their culture and their thinking and tap into workers' brains" (Hoerr, 1990).

## THE BACKLASH

Changes as sweeping and all-encompassing as the implementation of self-directed teams never occur without resistance. Here is a sampling of reactions to work teams that you will no doubt hear at one time or another.

## "Work teams are a foreign concept; they won't work in this country."

JOHN BRODIC, president of United Paperworkers Local 448, said in *Business Week,* "What the company wants is for us to work like the Japanese. Everybody go out and do jumping jacks in the morning and kiss each other when they go home at night. You work as a team, rat on each other, and lose control of your destiny. That's not going to work in this country" (Hoerr, 1989). Indeed, some Japanese concepts might *not* work here—but most do. The relevant fact is that empowered teams are not a foreign concept; they are compatible with American values and culture.

## "The concept is great, but the execution is lousy."

IN OTHER CASES, poor implementations can foster negative feelings. In the same *Business Week* article just mentioned, one auto worker complained that the initial team training sessions prepared everyone for increased levels of involvement in decision making, but when the factory hit full production, "all of a sudden, you were just another factory rat." A supervisor in another organization told us that he was called into a meeting with other supervisors where they all were informed that they would be moving to teams and their jobs would be phased out. The shocked group of supervisors was then asked to give support to the implementation.

## "It would have worked, but the managers and supervisors ruined everything."

NEGATIVE FEELINGS about teams will by no means be limited to line employees. Managers and supervisors can be significant obstacles to successful work team implementations. They have the most to lose in terms of status, authority, and power. In our experience, supervisors and managers reported being most threatened when work team practitioners started neglecting their responsibilities, creating role vacuums that caused these supervisors and managers to behave in all sorts of defensive and unproductive ways.

## "We tried teams, but employees wouldn't accept the change."

THIS COULD BE THE MOST damaging kind of backlash. "Let's go back to managers doing the managing and employees doing the work," some will say. There are situations in which employees are reluctant, for any number of reasons, to take on management and leadership responsibilities. The natural reaction of threatened managers will be, "I told you so." In most cases, however, these failures will not be due to continually reluctant employees, but to poor change management.

## AVOIDING BACKLASH

This book has attempted to provide strategies and tactics for successful team implementations that can help you to minimize backlash. By way of summary, let's take a quick look back at some of the major points we've emphasized that can help you keep your teams from losing ground.

*Design careful, thoughtful, well-planned implementations.* Contrary to the beliefs of some, a manager cannot just walk in one day and announce that he or she has implemented empowered teams. A clearly communicated vision and implementation plan are critical to success.

*Set realistic goals.* Don't expect a 40 percent improvement in productivity overnight. You will only be setting yourself up for disappointment and your teams for feelings of failure. You will be far better off setting challenging but achievable goals that will allow team members to bask in their sense of accomplishment.

*Provide appropriate training.* Teams require entire new sets of skills, and new skills require training and coaching. Short-cut the training and you will jeopardize your implementation.

*Teams should be part of an overall strategy.* Be careful of the tendency to jump on the team bandwagon. Make sure that teams are "right" for your organization, in terms of both your business objectives and your culture.

*Always look back.* The concept of continuous improvement can and should be applied to your team implementation. It will not be perfect the first time around because you will be learning, and conditions will change constantly. Take time to evaluate and modify your progress.

## SUMMARY

If you are new to the team concept, we hope that this book has opened your eyes to the possibilities offered by empowerment. If you are about to start teams, our hope is that we have provided guidance to help you through your first implementation.

And if you have already instituted teams, *Empowered Teams* may be able to provide a snapshot of what is going on in other organizations. Perhaps there are some "best practices" you can adapt to your own company from the many contained here.

Whatever the case, we are all on the cusp of a brave new *work* world. We believe that empowered teams will not fade as other recent management theories and techniques have done. On the contrary, teams will be the way all of us—in present and future generations—approach our work and our workplace.

# APPENDIX

# SURVEY METHODOLOGY:
## A Study of Current
## Self-Directed Team Practices

The majority of quantitative data mentioned throughout this book come from a survey study conducted jointly by Development Dimensions International, the Association for Quality and Participation (AQP), and *Industry Week*.

## Survey Design

Two surveys were used to collect the data for the study. A "Team Survey" was aimed at people who were directly involved with team activities, such as team members, team leaders, supervisors, and consultants. The "Executive Survey," a shorter and more succinct version of the Team Survey, was targeted at senior-level managers.

The use of two surveys was intended to provide a broad picture of self-directed teams (SDTs) and to permit a comparison of both groups across a variety of issues. Because of the different survey formats, it was not possible to compare the groups on every question. Survey questions were formulated, reviewed, and tested with team experts and research design professionals.

Because organizations had many different kinds of teams (such as quality circles or employee involvement teams), it was important to make sure that the people completing the surveys were involved in actual SDTs. To screen respondents, this definition of SDTs was printed on both surveys:

> A self-directed team is a group of employees who have day-to-day responsibility for managing themselves and the work they do. Members of self-directed teams typically handle job assignments, plan and schedule work, make production-related decisions, and take action on problems. Employees on SDTs work with a minimum of direct supervision. Self-directed teams are not quality circles or cross-functional task groups.

Respondents were instructed to complete the questionnaire only if their teams closely matched this definition.

## Distribution

The Team Survey was distributed in several ways. Two hundred surveys were handed out at the 1990 AQP Spring Conference, which typically draws 3,500 participants from the employee involvement and quality fields. Additional surveys were mailed to participants in other AQP conferences and training courses and to individuals who had recently purchased an AQP video on SDTs. A few surveys were sent to people suggested by consultants who were known for their work with SDTs.

The Executive Survey was mailed to a stratified random sample of 3,785 upper-level managers subscribing to *Industry Week*. With most of its subscribers in middle- to upper-level management positions, *Industry Week* provided a representative base from which to draw an executive perspective on SDTs. The sample was drawn from a list of titles, which included senior human resource managers, plant managers, and senior line managers, and which represented diverse geographic locations.

## Return Rates

Of the 1,108 Team Surveys distributed by mail and in person, 272 were completed, providing a response rate of 25 percent. Because there were few differences in the responses of the various groups that comprised the Team Survey sample (AQP conference attendees, consultant clients, etc.), the data were grouped together in the analysis. Of the 862 respondents to the Executive Survey, 232 indicated that they currently had at least one SDT in their organization.

## Types of Organizations in the Sample

The most prevalent type of organization represented in the Team Survey sample was manufacturing (71 percent). Fewer than half of these organizations (39 percent) reported a union affiliation. Other types of organizations included service (10 percent), public utilities (5 percent), and the military (3 percent). This distribution was not surprising; SDTs have been introduced primarily in manufacturing, and the majority of the surveys were sent to manufacturing organizations. In the Executive Survey sample, 95 percent of the respondents were from manufacturing settings; of these, 53 percent reported a union affiliation.

## Sizes of Organizations in the Sample

The organizations in the Team Survey sample ranged from relatively small companies of fewer than 100 employees (10 percent) to very large organizations of between 1,000 and 200,000 employees (37 percent); one-fourth of the respondents were from companies with 20,000 to 75,000 employees. The organizations represented in the Executive Survey sample averaged between 1,000 and 5,000 employees.

## The Respondents

The largest number of respondents to the Team Survey (41 percent) work as internal consultants or facilitators with SDTs in their organizations; thus, the Team Survey data primarily represent the views of these two groups. Also represented were team members (18 percent), first-line supervisors or group leaders (14 percent), team leaders (12 percent), and external consultants (6 percent).

Several respondents listed their roles in the "Other" category on the Team Survey. These included department heads, plant managers, senior managers, vice-presidents, operations managers, training managers, and team coordinators. Although the items listed in this category were too diverse to be considered representative of a given group, the range of responses highlighted the variety of roles and titles associated with SDTs.

More than half of the Team Survey respondents had two years' experience or less with SDTs in their organizations (62 percent). Thirty-eight percent had been working with SDTs for two or more years.

As expected, most of the Executive Survey respondents listed themselves as managers (41 percent), vice-presidents (26 percent), or directors (11 percent). These individuals were not asked to indicate the length of their experience with SDTs.

# ANNOTATED BIBLIOGRAPHY

W e have selected a number of articles that do an excellent job of presenting the team concept, reviewing results, and discussing implementation issues. Collectively, these articles would be very beneficial as a first-step orientation for those wanting to learn about teams.

Dumaine, B. "Who Needs a Boss?" *Fortune*, May 7, 1990, pp. 52–55, 58, 60.

Self-managed teams are reviewed in terms of their obstacles and successes, and Dumaine discusses the fact that work teams aren't for everyone. Of 476 Fortune 1,000 companies surveyed, only 7 percent are organized by work teams. However, half the companies stated that they will be relying on teams significantly in the future. Several comments from CEOs are quoted and key results cited. Implementations in companies like Federal Express Corporation and Johnsonville Foods are reviewed in detail.

Glickman, C. "Klear Knit Brings Back the Sewing Circle." *The Charlotte Observer*, Mar. 19, 1990, pp. 1D, 14D.

This article discusses how an apparel manufacturer is making the transformation to work teams, also called "modular manufacturing." At Klear Knit, members inspect each other's work, make quality improvement suggestions, and make decisions regarding starting and stopping production. Although the company has just begun its transformation, it has already reduced its reject rate to 0 percent, compared to a 25 percent average reject rate in line production. Other successful apparel manufacturers using this concept include Russel Corporation and Oxford Industries.

Hoerr, J. "Work Teams Can Rev Up Paper Pushers, Too." *Business Week*, Nov. 28, 1988, pp. 68–69.

Aid Association for Lutherans (AAL), a fraternal society that operates a huge insurance business, went through a three-year transformation to work teams. This transformation began in 1986 and by 1988 AAL was halfway to its goal of operating entirely with self-directed teams. In one year, the company increased productivity by 20 percent, reduced case-processing time by as much as 75 percent, and reduced personnel by 10 percent, while handling 10 percent more transactions. The article is an excellent case history of white-collar teams in action.

Hoerr, J. "The Payoff from Teamwork." *Business Week*, July 10, 1989, pp. 56–62.

This article views employee involvement as American industry's best hope for competing on an international level. It discusses the barriers to full worker participation—lack of government support, Wall Street's insistence on short-term results, and lack of union understanding and support. The article also discusses the difference between employee involvement in Japan and the United States. In the United States, workers tend to view participation as having a voice in all types of matters that in Japan are determined by management. Work team results cited include AT&T Credit Corporation's doubling of lease applications processed per day since moving to teams. General Electric Company's Salisbury, North Carolina, plant is also cited. The plant has increased productivity by 250 percent compared with other GE plants producing the same products.

Houston, P. "Timberrr!" *Business Month*, Dec. 1989, pp. 50–56.

Lake Superior Paper Industries (LSPI) is knocking down old barriers between labor and management and letting workers be their own bosses. In its first fiscal year, LSPI earned $3 million on revenues of $111 million, yet had predicted a $17 million loss. The article discusses how LSPI has made its thirty self-governing teams responsible for every aspect of operation, and it states that 98 percent of the problems in the system are caused by management. Top managers are having problems giving up control. They don't listen to suggestions from their employees and, as a result, have caused slowdowns in productivity.

Ketchum, L. D. "How Redesigned Plants Really Work." *National Productivity Review*, 1984, 3, 246–254.

Ketchum, a team pioneer, describes "work redesign" as a long-term, transformational process designed to comprehensively restructure workplaces into more productive and psychologically healthier organizations. He cites an example of a food product unit within a plant that exceeded every previous production and product quality achievement in only six weeks by focusing on whole process logic. Ketchum also describes work teams, including a typical team meeting. He provides supporting arguments for why redesigned organizations perform better—psychologically, economically, and technologically.

Lee, C. "Beyond Teamwork." *Training*, June 1990, pp. 25–32.

This article discusses the road to self-directed work teams, walking the reader through the basic stages and describing the distinguishable characteristics of teams. The rationale for going through the process of converting to work teams also is provided, and the author cautions would-be team converts: "The road to self-directed teams is littered with landmines. . . . Even the wary are liable to find the process uncomfortable, confusing, and excruciatingly slow" (p. 31). Several success stories are noted, including the Procter & Gamble Company, Johnsonville Foods, General Mills, Corning, and Aid Association for Lutherans. Lee also notes DDI's model of the self-directed work team continuum.

Moskal, B. S. "The Wizards of Buick City." *Industry Week*, May 7, 1990, pp. 22–28.

General Motors Corporation's Buick City plant is an excellent example of work team success. This article describes the trials and tribulations the plant underwent during its five-year shift to self-managed work teams. Buick City dealt with technical, interpersonal, and operational barriers in its shift to teams. In doing so, it reduced warranty costs, assembly hours, and absenteeism. The plant also improved the Buick LeSabre from being one of the lowest-quality-ranking cars in 1986 and 1987 to ranking number 1 in quality in 1989.

O'Dell, C. "Team Play, Team Pay—New Ways of Keeping Score." *Across the Board*, Nov. 1989, pp. 38–45.

This article discusses how and why organizational reward systems must be linked to team concepts. It stresses the need for companies to examine their performance appraisal and merit pay systems to ensure that they are not undermining teamwork. Suggestions for structuring reward systems that support team concepts are provided, and a number of company success stories are cited. Among the companies noted are AT&T Credit Corporation, Honeywell, Tennessee Eastman, General Electric Company, Motorola, and Xerox Corporation.

Proctor, B. H. "A Sociotechnical Work-Design System at Digital Enfield: Utilizing Untapped Resources." *National Productivity Review*, Summer 1986, pp. 262–270.

This article illustrates how DEC has achieved a leading edge in system integration and sociotechnical design. Digital's 200-employee plant at Enfield began design in 1981 and shipped its first product in April 1983. The plant is reviewed as a total system in which the human and technical elements are dealt with equally. Each of DEC's operating teams manages a business dedicated to building a product all the way from raw materials to shipping. There are three business units; each unit has one to four teams, and each team has twelve to eighteen members. Every team member is trained in each step of the building process, and a skill-based pay system rewards members. The DEC Enfield plant is one of the classic and highly successful examples of self-directed teams.

Semler, R. "Managing Without Managers." *Harvard Business Review*, Sept.–Oct. 1989, pp. 76–84.

Semco S/A is a machinery manufacturer in Brazil. The company went from near financial disaster in 1980 to a 10 percent sales profit margin in 1988. Semco's success is attributed to its ability to link democracy, profit sharing, and information to its operations. Semco designed an organizational circle to replace the traditional hierarchy, reduced management, formed work teams, and gave the teams free rein in the company. In one year sales doubled, the inventory cycle fell from 136 days to 46 days, rejection rates dropped, and productivity improved. It is the amazing story of an empowered work culture from abroad.

Sims, H. P., and Dean, J. W. "Beyond Quality Circles: Self-Managing Teams." *Personnel*, Jan. 1985, pp. 25–32.

Sims and Dean consider self-managing teams the logical extension of quality circles. The article reviews the quality circle concept, why managers like it, and its limitations. Self-managing teams are reviewed in terms of their benefits, as well as the reasons why adoption of the concept has been slow. A specific comparison of quality circles and self-managed teams is provided, and the article concludes with a brief look at the resources required for team development.

Thompson D. B. "Everybody's a Boss." *Industry Week*, Feb. 23, 1987, pp. 16–17.

This article discusses the success the Goodyear Tire and Rubber Company had using the team concept at their Lawton, Oklahoma, facility. Goodyear employed a two-phase approach, first forming 164 teams with a cross-section of skills, and then creating "business centers" within each work group. Each group is responsible for its own goals, productivity costs, waste, and so on. The plant operates with 35 percent fewer managers and is producing 50,000 tires per day compared with 25,000 at a similar plant.

Walton, R. E. "Work Innovations at Topeka: After Six Years." *The Journal of Applied Behavioral Science*, 1979, *13* (3), 422–433.

The Gaines dog food plant in Topeka, Kansas, is one of the earliest work team sites in the United States. This article reviews the first six years of the plant's operation by focusing on significant events during the five phases of team development. The difficulties facing management are emphasized, yet the author points out that these difficulties can be avoided. The plant operated nearly four years without a lost time accident, has realized savings of millions of dollars annually, and has been the model for similar work innovations in other plants.

Walton, R. E. ''From Control to Commitment in the Workplace.'' *Harvard Business Review*, Mar.–Apr. 1985, pp. 77–84.

Walton, in this widely quoted article, provides a solid explanation of the self-directed team concept, including an analysis of the cooperative approach of SDTs as compared to the traditional control strategy. The emphasis on teams within an organization should be to continually improve, stretch objectives, reflect requirements in the marketplace, and pursue the challenge of giving employees assurance of job security and voice. Pioneers of self-directed teams include General Foods, General Motors Corporation, Cummins Engine Company, and the Procter & Gamble Company. These companies have reported boosts in quality, lower absenteeism and turnovers, and reductions in operating and support costs.

# REFERENCES

Blines, D. "Semi-autonomous Team in the Zoo." *The Journal for Quality and Participation*, July–Aug. 1990, pp. 93–95.

Byham, W. C. *Applying a Systems Approach to Personnel Activities.* Monograph IX. Pittsburgh, Pa.: Development Dimensions International, 1987.

Byham, W. C. *Zapp! The Lightning of Empowerment.* New York: Harmony Books, 1990.

Carnevale, A. P., Gainer, L. J., and Meltzer, A. S. *Workplace Basics: The Skills Employers Want.* American Society for Training and Development and U.S. Department of Labor Report 0-225-795-QL.2. Washington, D.C.: U.S. Government Printing Office, 1988.

Cherns, A. "The Principles of Socio-Technical Design." *Human Relations*, 1976, *29*, pp. 783–792.

Cherry, R. "The Development of General Motors' Team-Based Plants in the Innovative Organization." In R. Zager and M. P. Rosow (eds.), *The Innovative Organization: Productivity Programs in Action*, pp. 125–148. New York: Pergamon, 1982.

Dumaine, B. "Who Needs a Boss?" *Fortune*, May 7, 1990, pp. 52–55, 58, 60.

Echols, D., and Mitchell, R. "Champion or Victim? The Supervisor's New Role in a Team-Based Work System." Paper presented at Seventh Annual Fall Forum, Association for Quality and Participation, Denver, Colo., Oct. 1990.

Emery, F. E. "Designing Socio-Technical Systems for Greenfield Sites." *Journal of Occupational Behavior*, 1980, *1*, 19–27.

Gladstein, D. L. "Groups in Context: A Model of Task Group Effectiveness." *Administrative Science Quarterly*, 1984, *29*, 499–517.

Gwynne, S. C. "The Right Stuff." *Time*, Oct. 29, 1990, pp. 74–84.

Hackman, J. R. "The Design of Work Teams." In J. Lorsch (ed.), *Handbook of Organizational Behavior.* Englewood Cliffs, N.J.: Prentice-Hall, 1987.

Hackman, J. R. (ed.). *Groups That Work (And Those That Don't): Creating Conditions for Effective Teamwork.* San Francisco: Jossey-Bass, 1989.

Hauenstein, P., and Byham, W. C. *Understanding Job Analysis.* Monograph XI. Pittsburgh, Pa.: Development Dimensions International, 1989.

Hoerr, J. "Getting Man and Machine to Live Happily Ever After." *Business Week,* Apr. 20, 1987, pp. 61–62.

Hoerr, J. "Work Teams Can Rev Up Paper Pushers, Too." *Business Week,* Nov. 28, 1988, pp. 68–69.

Hoerr, J. "The Cultural Revolution at A. O. Smith." *Business Week,* May 29, 1989a, pp. 66–68.

Hoerr, J. "The Payoff from Teamwork." *Business Week,* July 10, 1989b, pp. 56–62.

Hoerr, J. "Sharpening Minds for a Competitive Edge." *Business Week,* Dec. 17, 1990, pp. 72–78.

Hoerr, J., and Pollock, M. A. "Management Discovers the Human Side of Automation." *Business Week,* Sept. 29, 1986, pp. 74–77.

Howard, R. "Values Make the Company." *Harvard Business Review,* Sept.–Oct. 1990, pp. 132–145.

Jessup, H. R. "New Roles in Team Leadership." *Training and Development Journal,* Nov. 1990, pp. 79–83.

Johnson, R. "Volvo's New Assembly Plant Has No Assembly Line." *Automotive News,* July 10, 1989, pp. 22, 24.

Katz, D., and Kahn, R. L. *The Social Psychology of Organization.* (2nd ed.) New York: Wiley, 1978.

Ketchum, L. D. "How Redesigned Plants Really Work." *National Productivity Review,* 1984, 3, 246–254.

Lawler III, E. E. *High-Involvement Management: Participative Strategies for Improving Organizational Performance.* San Francisco: Jossey-Bass, 1986.

Ledford, G. E. *The Design of Skill-Based Pay Plans.* COE Pub. 689-15. Los Angeles: University of Southern California, Center for Effective Organization, 1989.

Lee, C. "Beyond Teamwork." *Training,* June 1990, pp. 25–32.

Macy, B. A., Norton, J. J., Bliese, P. O., and Izumi, H. "The Bottom Line Impact of New Design and the Design: North America from 1961–1990." Paper presented at International Conference on Self-Managed Work Teams, Denton, Tex., Sept. 1990.

Manz, C. C., and Sims, H. P., Jr. *Superleadership: Leading Others to Lead Themselves.* Englewood Cliffs, N.J.: Prentice-Hall, 1989.

Moskal, B. S. "Is Industry Ready for Adult Relationships?" *Industry Week,* Jan. 21, 1991, pp. 18–27.

National Center of Education and the Economy. *America's Choice: High Skills or Low Wages.* Rochester, N.Y.: National Center of Education and the Economy, 1990.

Near, R., and Weckler, D. "Organizational and Job Characteristics Related to Self-Managing Teams." Paper presented at International Conference on Self-Managed Work Teams, Denton, Tex., Sept. 1990.

O'Dell, C. "Team Play, Team Pay—New Ways of Keeping Score." *Across the Board,* Nov. 1989, pp. 38–45.

Parker, M., and Slaughter, J. *Choosing Sides: Unions and the Team Concept.* Boston: South End Press, 1988.

Patinkin, M. "Gamble on Assembly Teams Pays Off." *Pittsburgh Press,* 1987, pp. B6–B7.

Robenstein, S. "Don't Fear the Team, Join It." *New York Times,* June 11, 1989, s. 3, p. 2.

Semler, R. "Managing Without Managers." *Harvard Business Review,* Sept.–Oct. 1989, pp. 76–84.

Sheridan, J. H. "America's Best Plants." *Industry Week,* Oct. 1990, pp. 27–64.

Stayer, R. "How I Learned to Let My Workers Lead." *Harvard Business Review,* Nov.–Dec. 1990, pp. 66–83.

Sundstrom, E., Demeuse, K., and Futrell, D. "Work Teams: Applications and Effectiveness." *American Psychologist,* Feb. 1990, pp. 120–133.

Taylor, F. *Principles of Scientific Management.* New York: Harper & Row, 1947.

Toffler, A. *Powershift: Knowledge, Wealth, and Violence at the Edge of the Twenty-First Century.* New York: Bantam Books, 1990.

Trist, E. *The Evolution of Socio-technical Systems.* Occasional paper No. 2. Toronto: Quality of Working Life Centre, 1981.

Verespej, M. A. "Yea, Teams? Not Always." *Industry Week,* June 18, 1990, pp. 103–105.

Walton, R. E. "Work Innovations at Topeka: After Six Years." *The Journal of Applied Behavioral Science,* 1979, *13* (3), 422–433.

Walton, R. E. "From Control to Commitment in the Workplace." *Harvard Business Review,* Mar.–Apr. 1985, pp. 77–84.

Wellins, R. S., Wilson, J., Katz, A. J., Laughlin, P., and Day, C. R., Jr. *Self-Directed Teams: A Study of Current Practice.* Survey report. Pittsburgh, Pa.: Development Dimensions International, Association for Quality and Participation, and *Industry Week,* 1990.

Wesner, M., and Egan, C. "Self-Managed Teams in Operator Services." Paper presented at International Conference on Self-Managed Work Teams, Denton, Tex., Sept. 1990.

"What Workers Want: The Gap in Management's Perception." *Behavioral Sciences Newsletter,* June 27, 1988, p. 1.

Wysocki, L. "Implementation of Self-Managed Teams Within a Non-union Manufacturing Facility." Paper presented at International Conference on Self-Managed Work Teams, Denton, Tex., Sept. 1990.

# INDEX

*Page numbers in italics refer to figures. Page numbers followed by "t" refer to tables.*